* * * * * * *

A NEW DEAL FOR
LATIN AMERICA

* * * * * * *

A NEW DEAL FOR LATIN AMERICA

LATIN AMERICA

The Alliance for Progress

* * * * * * * * * * * * *

LINCOLN GORDON

UNITED STATES AMBASSADOR TO BRAZIL

HARVARD UNIVERSITY PRESS

CAMBRIDGE, MASSACHUSETTS · 1963

338.91
266w

Distributed in Great Britain by Oxford University Press • London

Library of Congress Catalog Card Number: 63–13812

Printed in the United States of America

F H

CONTENTS

* * * * * * * * * * * * *

* * * * * * *

A NEW DEAL FOR
LATIN AMERICA

* * * * * * *

FOREWORD

Rio de Janeiro · December 1962

* * * * * * * * * * * * *

This book is based on a series of addresses delivered by me before various audiences in Brazil during the first ten months of my service as United States Ambassador, from October 1961 to August 1962. The addresses were intended to explain the philosophy, purposes, and working methods of the Alliance for Progress, to analyze difficulties and obstacles confronting the program, and to dispel certain widely held misunderstandings.

The material has been edited to remove purely local or topical references. Although specific examples of projects or problems are naturally drawn from experience in Brazil, the main substance of the book is concerned with the Alliance for Progress as it affects the whole of Latin America.*

* Similar versions of the same addresses, together with one before the Brazilian National War College in May 1962 on "American Foreign Policy: The Cold War and Latin America," were published in Portuguese in October 1962. See Lincoln Gordon, *O Progresso pela Aliança* (Rio de Janeiro: Distribuidora Récord).

The idea of the Alliance for Progress was launched in an address by President John F. Kennedy to Latin American representatives assembled in the White House on March 13, 1961. It at once became the subject of active discussion in all the capitals of this Hemisphere. The Council of the Organization of American States (OAS) promptly resolved that it should be considered by a special meeting of the Inter-American Economic and Social Council at Ministerial level. This meeting took place from August 5 to 17, 1961, at Punta del Este, Uruguay, where the national delegations were led by Ministers of Finance or Economy (in the case of the United States by the Secretary of the Treasury). Out of this meeting there emerged the basic documents of the Alliance—the Declaration to the Peoples of America and the Charter of Punta del Este—which are reprinted in the appendix to this book.

These were truly multilateral agreements, reflecting a consensus of all the signatory delegations (i.e., all of the twenty-one American republics except Cuba) and taking into account suggestions from all quarters. The agenda and the background papers for the Conference had been prepared by special working groups organized by the OAS Assistant Secretary General for Economic and Social Affairs, Dr. Jorge Sol, together with the President of the Inter-American Development Bank, Dr. Felipe Herrera, and the Executive Secretary of the United Nations Economic Commission for Latin America (ECLA), Dr. Raúl Prebisch.

The Alliance for Progress is a major undertaking in inter-American collaboration for sustained economic and social progress in Latin America. It is by far the most ambitious such undertaking ever subscribed to by the Western Hemisphere governments. But its concepts were not suddenly born in the year 1961. As a member of President-elect Kennedy's Task Force on Latin American Policy in late 1960 and an active participant in the advance preparations and the discussions at the Conference of Punta del Este, I can state with authority that earlier Latin American thinking on the causes of economic underdevelopment and the measures most likely to accelerate both economic and social progress was of the greatest possible influence in the formulation of current United States policies. The Alliance for Progress grew directly out of the background of years of analysis by the Inter-American Economic and Social Council and the U.N. Economic Commission for Latin America, and out of a series of policy proposals by various Latin American statesmen and other leaders of opinion.

Among those policy proposals, the initiative of Brazilian President Juscelino Kubitschek in May 1958 for "Operation Pan America" was of special importance, as is recognized in the very title of the Charter of Punta del Este. It gave a new impetus to inter-American cooperation in the economic and social fields. Its first concrete results were the creation in 1959 of the Inter-American Development Bank, in response to a long-held desire of Latin American governments, and the adoption in September 1960 of the Act of Bogotá, with the subsequent creation by the United States of a special fund of 500 million dollars to assist accelerated social progress in the Hemisphere. The proposal for Operation Pan America was the seed from which the Alliance for Progress took its origin.

In its first year, the Alliance has enjoyed many successes, but it has also encountered many obstacles and engendered some disappointments. There has been official discussion in the inter-American family of a "crisis" in the Alliance.* Many of the obstacles and disappointments are commented on in the chapters that follow. The mood of self-analysis and constructive criticism is a healthy one. There is certainly ample scope for improvement in organization and structure, in working methods both in Latin America and in the United States, in arrangements for collaboration by other capital-supplying nations and international institutions, and above all in the multilateral political impetus required to make the program a success.

The success of the Alliance for Progress is, in my opinion, indispensable to the future of political liberty, as well as material prosperity, in this Hemisphere. I believe that the basic concepts of the Charter of Punta del Este are sound, and that they deserve the close attention and full support of enlightened opinion in the

* See Organization of American States, Inter-American Economic and Social Council, First Annual Meeting at the Ministerial Level, *Report of the Panel of Experts to the Inter-American Economic and Social Council*, Washington, September 1962.

free world. I hope that this small book may make some contribution to a better public understanding of this program for constructive democratic revolution in the Hemisphere—for a true "new deal" in Latin America.

I

PURPOSES OF THE
ALLIANCE FOR PROGRESS

*   *   *   *   *   *   *   *   *   *   *   *   *

What is the Alliance for Progress? In a single sentence, it is a sustained and cooperative effort to accelerate economic growth and social progress throughout Latin America, working through democratic institutions based on respect for the individual.

In this effort the United States is prepared to devote very large amounts of public resources. Over the ten years now envisaged, those resources will be comparable in dollar amount to what went into the Marshall Plan for Western Europe's postwar economic recovery. The total outside resources available for Latin America should far exceed the Marshall Plan magnitudes. The United States Congress has shown vigorous support for this program on the condition that it meets in practice the high standards subscribed to by twenty American republics in the Charter of Punta del Este on August 17, 1961.*

* For text see page 118.

This must be a sustained effort because the nature of the task is a long and hard one—much longer and harder than that of European postwar recovery. Much of Latin America, alongside its great cities like Rio de Janeiro, São Paulo, and Buenos Aires, suffers from deep poverty and technical backwardness in the countryside, from glaring deficiencies in education, housing, and public health, from explosive forces of population increase, and from weaknesses in economic and administrative structures which must be remedied to release the vast potentials of this continent for rapid growth. Democratic institutions in Latin America are on trial as never before to test their capacity to meet the demands imposed upon them for social and economic progress.

The Alliance for Progress must be a cooperative effort. Without the enthusiastic devotion of Latin American talents, energies, and resources to its purposes, no lasting results can be achieved. We on the outside can supplement and complement domestic efforts; we can and will help financially and technically; but our efforts cannot substitute for those generated from within. Nor is this Alliance merely a matter of bilateral cooperation between the United States and each Latin American nation. It calls for a major part to be played by inter-American institutions, by the world-wide international agencies, and by the other more industrialized countries able to help. The program includes international cooperation for the strengthening of certain commodity markets, notably that of coffee. It also looks to a strengthening of economic ties within Latin America through free trade areas and common markets and through reinforced cooperation in science, research, and specialized education.

In all these fields, Brazil can and should have a major role of leadership. Indeed, the Alliance for Progress is much the same in principle as the Brazilian idea of Operation Pan America, and I have thought that the program now underway might well be called "Operation Alliance."

The Alliance for Progress emphasizes the twin goals of economic development and social progress. These goals are Siamese twins. Production and living standards in Latin America are low—very much lower than could be secured from the available physical and human resources and the known techniques of production. Without higher production, which means economic development, the people cannot enjoy decent standards of nutrition, health, clothing, housing, education—the material foundations for human dignity. Higher production requires public and private capital investment, new agricultural techniques, more industrialization, expansion of exports, and all the other elements of economic modernization. But mere increases in production will not suffice unless their benefits are widely distributed among all classes of societies and among all regions of the nation. Nor will development meet the ultimate tests of success unless all sectors of society feel themselves to be full participants in the process of development. The concept of the Alliance for Progress does not permit the continued existence of large masses of "forgotten men."

In these respects, the Alliance for Progress fits squarely with the precepts of the recent Papal Encyclical *Mater et Magistra*. As one reads the teachings of that Encyclical, one is struck by the fact that the Western World in its most developed parts has come closer to achieving its noble aspirations than any other society today or at any time in history. Our system of education comes closer to meeting the ideal of true equality of opportunity. Our system of labor relations comes closer to harmonizing the interests of manual workers, salaried employees, managers, and owners in the common goals of high production and broad distribution of goods and services. Our systems of progressive taxation and guaranteed social security come closer to insuring that all share equitably in the public burdens and that none of our citizens is left bypassed by the tides of economic and social change. We have many deficiencies and much to improve, and we advertise our deficiencies widely through a free press whose very existence is an assurance that corrective efforts will be made.

We have accomplished all this without paternalism by a few, without concentration of power in irresponsible hands, and without the infernal mechanisms of a police state creating a false image of harmony and popular support, manufactured to suit a dictatorial elite which makes colonial subjects of its own peoples. Contrast this with the new tyrannies which must build concrete walls topped by barbed wire and policed by floodlights, machine guns, and tanks to keep their dissatisfied citizens from escaping what their masters brazenly describe as an earthly paradise.

It is not the purpose of the Alliance for Progress to impose a North American way of life on Latin America. We know that each Latin American nation has its own cultural traditions and potentials, that each will find its own social forms and expressions, and that the world will be enriched by their diversity and their mutual interchange. But in this diversity there is one constant: the common devotion to democratic institutions and respect for the human individual. Latin America has had its fill of dictatorships, Brazil fortunately suffering less from them than most of her Spanish-speaking neighbors. It is our common purpose to demonstrate that free institutions can and will meet the material needs of men working together through methods and leaders of their own choosing.

Let me comment briefly on the methods to be used in the Alliance for Progress. There are two points of special importance: systematic planning for economic and social development, and the principle of self-help and institutional reform.

As the Charter of Punta del Este makes clear, development planning does not mean socialization. What it does mean is the establishment of targets for public investment in fields of high priority (and by implication the elimination of those of low or no priority); the application of sound engineering and economic standards to public investment projects; an appraisal of the balance-of-payments problems involved in the program; the provision of adequate machinery for public administration and for cooperation between government and private organizations; and the adoption of fiscal and monetary policies to promote development without inflation.

Without this kind of program, the effort for accelerated development will be undermined by the squandering of limited resources on low-priority uses, by the encouragement of inflationary pressures, and by the incapacity of administrative machinery to do what is needed. None of us familiar with Latin American history during recent years need think very hard to find dramatic and painful examples of these failings. Nor can development planning be merely on paper; it must be geared to the budget and to the real centers of decision-making in the operating ministries and other agencies controlling investment funds.

A sound development program is itself a major element in the concept of self-help and institutional reform. I stressed earlier that outside resources, though indispensable, can only supplement domestic Latin American efforts for development. Self-help means both an adequate contribution of domestic resources to the needs of high priority and the carrying through of necessary structural improvements in such fields as land tenure, tax systems and tax administration, educational institutions, capital markets, and the machinery of public administration. It means systematic efforts to stimulate savings and their application to investments essential to national growth.

Brazil today, like many other countries, is beset with grievous day-to-day difficulties in the rising cost of living, in labor relations, and in other fields. We do not look for miracles. In the immediate task of economic stabilization, we are providing substantial assistance, but we also know that although stabilization is imperative, it will not by itself solve all the urgent problems confronting the nation. We also recognize that economic underdevelopment implies some degree of administrative underdevelopment, and one aspect of the program is designed to provide needed technicians and training programs to build up the cadres of specialized technical personnel which are still woefully inadequate in most of Latin America. The target is not perfection, but rather clear and consistent movement in the desired direction so that visible progress can be made in short order.

Nor is the Alliance for Progress purely a matter of cooperation among *governments*. If its goals are to be reached, a very large part will have to be played by private enterprise—Latin American, foreign, and perhaps especially joint ventures. If in recent years there has been an unfortunate and widespread error in assuming that private enterprise alone could bring about adequate development in Latin America, we should not now overcompensate that error by assuming that private enterprise is of little importance. In the vast bulk of manufacturing, mining, agriculture, commerce, and finance, private enterprise is the dominant and the most productive form of economic organization. These sectors cannot move forward without new investment, new techniques, and more effective management. To all these needs, foreign companies have made and are continuing to make enormous contributions. To be welcome, a foreign enterprise must be fully a part of the community in which it operates, receiving a fair return for risks undertaken and for capital and technique imported from abroad, but providing its main economic benefits to the host country. The record shows that this has in fact been the case with the great majority of American foreign investments in Brazil. I only wish that sometimes the investing companies devoted more effort to letting the facts—facts on their provision of jobs, of training, of payrolls, of taxes paid, and of profits reinvested—be more widely known.

Finally, why is the United States interested in the Alliance for Progress? Why should our Congress, acting on behalf of us taxpayers, be committing large resources to this effort? The answer lies in the conviction that a prosperous, free, and self-reliant Latin America is essential to the kind of world in which we of the northern part of the Hemisphere can also pursue our aspirations for a life in freedom and dignity. This is not a mere matter of economic arithmetic, although we also know that prosperous neighbors make good trading partners. Nor is it a matter of political arithmetic; we know that real allies cannot be bought and we welcome the voluntary cooperation of our Latin American friends in world affairs because we share the same views toward peace and freedom in the world.

The basic reason is that we know that the United States cannot survive as an isolated island of prosperity in a shrinking world in which large numbers of people lack the essentials for a decent life. We know that our own future is indissolubly linked with the success or failure of this common effort. The human qualities of peoples such as the Brazilians, and the potential resources at their disposal, give us confidence that they will find the ways to overcome the obstacles of the present and to assure for themselves in measurable time the bright and free future which is their just desert.

2

BENEFITS FOR THE
BRAZILIAN PEOPLE

* * * * * * * * * * * * *

Some time ago, when I was still a private citizen, a distinguished member of the United States Senate who was visiting Brazil for the first time asked my advice whether he should go to São Paulo. He said that he had heard that it was the Chicago of South America, and he saw no reason to visit a second Chicago. Because I knew São Paulo, both as a symbol of dynamic economic progress and as a world-famous cultural center, I told him that he must see São Paulo, and he did. I saw him just after his return. Full of enthusiasm, he said that it was an injustice to liken São Paulo to Chicago. He found São Paulo a quite superior city, except for the absence of Lake Michigan, and he thought that Paulista energy might even create a second Lake Michigan if the residents were so inclined. (Perhaps I should add that the Senator is not from the State of Illinois.)

Keeping in mind São Paulo's forceful but disciplined energy as an illustration of what Brazilians are capable of, let us examine the broader question of economic and social development in Brazil and how "Operation Alliance" may be related to it. I suggested this term earlier, not only to show the intimate relationship between the Brazilian proposal for Operation Pan America and President Kennedy's proposal for an Alliance for Progress, but also to emphasize that the program adopted at Punta del Este is intended to be truly operational—to produce concrete results in measurable time. And I discuss this theme not only as the Ambassador of a friendly nation which places the highest hopes on the future of Brazil, but also as a professor and student of economic development.

The Declaration of Punta del Este described the Alliance for Progress as "a vast effort to bring a better life to all the peoples of the Continent," working through democratic institutions for accelerated economic and social development. The Charter of Punta del Este sets forth targets for economic and social progress and outlines ways and means of achieving these targets through national development programs, institutional improvements, and the mobilization of public and private resources for these purposes from within Latin America, and from North American and other outside sources, on a very large scale. The Declaration and Charter deserve the most careful study by any citizen of the Americas truly interested in the progress of his country and the hemisphere.*

Brazil has enjoyed an impressive degree of economic growth during the years since the Second World War, in large part focused on the City and State of São Paulo. But this is only a beginning. With a high rate of population growth, with a continuous movement of people from countryside to cities, Brazil has a need for development that is never-ending, whether viewed in terms of jobs for the growing labor force or in terms of needs and desires of the people for a truly modern standard of living. There are the urgent social problems of inadequate housing, inadequate educational opportunities, and of water supply, sanitation, and other requisites for public health. There are the structural problems of land tenure, of capital markets, of stronger democratic trade unions, of farmers' cooperatives, and of other needed institutional improvements. And there are the all-pervasive and interrelated problems of combatting inflation, which undermines the nation's vitality, and of expanding and diversifying Brazilian exports and replacing imports so that the chronic weakness of the balance of payments can be overcome.

I suppose that all Brazilians would agree on these objectives, which are also the objectives of Operation Alliance. The question remains: which road is to be followed toward this necessary process of development?

* Texts of these documents begin on page 113.

Development is indispensable to meet the material aspirations of the people. Development is also indispensable because only through greater production and greater productivity can the legitimate claims of social groups and regions within a nation be harmonized instead of degenerating into class warfare and regional warfare. But it should be development with a heart—development with a just distribution of its benefits—and development with full participation by all sectors of the community.

The two keys to development are investment and improved knowledge and technique. Improved knowledge and technique require human investment through education and training and research, forms of investment which, as recent studies demonstrate, provide returns, even in purely material terms, exceeding those of most physical investment.

Investment, in turn, requires savings, either voluntary or forced, domestic or foreign. It is here that the possible roads to development diverge. There is the road of free institutions, toward which the Alliance for Progress points. And there is the Soviet road.

Voices are heard suggesting that the road for Latin American countries to follow toward economic and social development is the totalitarian road marked out by Soviet Russia. Without significant foreign capital, it is said, the Soviet Union has transformed itself into a leading industrial nation in a period of thirty to forty years.

Let us examine that experience. Russia had its first important phase of industrial growth before the First World War with the help of substantial foreign credits. Then war and Communist revolution came to Russia, and the second great phase of industrial expansion was launched under Stalin's dictatorship with the series of five-year plans beginning in the late 1920's. The capital for that industrialization was squeezed from the peasantry through collectivization, which was enforced by deporting some five million peasants to Siberia, and through the seizure of grain from the collective farms, which led to the starvation—perhaps one should say the liquidation—of millions of Soviet citizens. This may seem difficult to believe, but the fact is there. Industrial productivity was also spurred by the threat of exile to forced labor camps in Siberia, and a portion of the industrialization was carried out directly by forced labor.

Thirty years later, Russia had built an impressive structure of heavy industry, but its products were still going largely into military uses and into further investment, so that consumption levels remained where they had been in the 1920's. Still today, the standards of housing are below those of Latin America, to say nothing of Western Europe and North America. Agricultural productivity remains a small fraction of the levels prevailing in the great agricultural areas of the free world.

One can be impressed with certain aspects of Soviet science and technical education, with the steel mills, nuclear rockets, and space satellites. But would any free nation want to build its industry by forced labor and by the collectivization and starvation of its farmers? Would any free people willingly subject themselves to the inhuman terror which for twenty-seven years replaced belief in God by belief in Stalin, who is now denounced by his own successors and whose body has been removed from Lenin's tomb perhaps to make room for some other deified ruler?

Contrast this with the free road to development. This is not the road of unbridled individualism, for free institutions need not imply the absence of planning and direction. It is the road of individual energies channeled by institutions responsible to the people and adapted to the needs of the society and the times. The free road is not simply the road of Western Europe or the United States in the nineteenth century, or of Canada or Australia in the twentieth century, though all these cases contain much that is useful.

Some observers say that the experience of the recently settled Anglo-Saxon countries is not relevant to the problems of Brazil, with its Latin traditions and its problems of land tenure inherited from centuries of plantation society. I call their attention to the Italian experience of recent years.

Italy too is a Latin country, small in size compared to Brazil but with many resemblances. It has a mountainous and difficult terrain. For generations its South has been a depressed area like Brazil's Northeast. Italy lacks adequate fuel resources. It has a great industrial center in

Milan remarkably similar to that of its Brazilian sister city of São Paulo. It has suffered from inflation and from long periods of economic stagnation. It has had a desperate problem of unemployment which in the early years of the Marshall Plan seemed incurable.

Despite these obstacles, Italian industrial production has more than doubled since 1953, increasing last year alone by 15 percent. Gross production has increased by 7½ percent a year. The specter of unemployment no longer looms as a threat to social and political stability. And Italy's balance of international payments today is one of the strongest in the world.

How has this been done? By a combination of sound financial policy which gave Italy ten years of stable prices, the vigorous promotion of domestic and foreign private investment, the careful planning of public investment with special emphasis on the depressed South, the fruitful application of foreign assistance from the United States and elsewhere, the opening up of Italian enterprise to competitive stimulus through the European common market, the expansion and diversification of exports, and the modernization of management and labor skills through education, training, and the stimulation of higher productivity.

In all of the cases of free world development, public investment and private investment have worked side by side; domestic investment and foreign investment have worked side by side; and development has brought about higher consumption levels, a more even distribution of income, and a broader integration into the peaceful international economic community.

Fifteen years ago, many Italian entrepreneurs were convinced that the Italian market was inherently limited, and that their only hope for profitable business was to maintain entrenched monopolistic positions protected from foreign and domestic competition alike. They believed in a small volume of production with very high profit margins on each unit sold. Now they have learned that an expanding economy can give them a larger domestic market, based on large volume and low profit margins per unit.

The factory parking lots, once containing only bicycles, have been enlarged to accommodate the passenger cars of the workers. Southern peasants, who used to accept ill health and miserable living conditions as the permanent lot of mankind, now are beginning to get decent housing and to find, through education, opportunities for their children which would have seemed unbelievable a generation ago. At the same time, the markets for makers of building materials, household and consumer goods, vehicles, and the tools and machinery which go to make these goods are expanding as never before. And all this was achieved in the face of concerted and destructive efforts by the large Italian Communist Party to sabotage the Marshall Plan, the Italian plan for reconstruction of the South, and the entire drive of the Italian nation for economic and social progress along the free road to development.

The Alliance for Progress does not imply leaving development to the automatic forces of the market. On the contrary, it recognizes the need for an intensive and systematic effort for the planned acceleration of development, with priority for the most urgent social and economic tasks. It is this systematic planning effort—the selection of priorities and the joint application of domestic and outside resources to these tasks—which constitutes the core idea of the Alliance for Progress.

These principles are not new to the State of São Paulo. They can be seen at work in the Plan of Action of the present state government, with its harmonious interweaving of public and private investment, its balancing of economic and social objectives, and its recognition of the need for administrative and institutional improvement, including agrarian reform. Other regions of Brazil are less fortunately endowed with resources, but their problems are not insoluble if similar principles are applied. São Paulo itself has a great role to play in this national effort. I am greatly impressed with its public and private recognition of the need to participate actively in the development of Brazil's North and Northeast. Just as São Paulo recognizes the importance to itself of a prospering national environment, so do we in the United States recognize our own need for a healthy environment in the Hemisphere as a whole.

In this connection, let me comment on some curious myths concerning United States policy toward Latin American development. One is that we seek to depress the prices of Latin American exports, such as coffee, and to raise the prices of our exports to Latin America. But, as is generally known, coffee is in world oversupply, and Brazil has been losing an important share of its market to African competitors. The United States, far from encouraging lower prices, has helped to negotiate the present international coffee agreement, and in accordance with the Charter of Punta del Este is now working side by side with Brazilian representatives for a stronger agreement to ensure against a disastrous collapse of the world coffee market. And on the other side of the terms of trade, sellers of industrial tools and machinery from various countries are competing vigorously to obtain orders from Brazil and other developing countries.

Then there is the myth about American efforts to retard Latin American industrialization in order to maintain our own export markets. This idea shares a kind of uneasy coexistence in some Latin American minds with the feeling that there is too much United States participation in Latin American industrialization. Perhaps the two thoughts cancel each other out. Actually, we welcome enthusiastically the industrial modernization of Brazil and of all Latin America. This is one of the explicit goals of the Alliance for Progress. The rapidly growing manpower of Latin America cannot be productively employed without massive industrialization, which is likewise essential to the achievement of balanced economies and to the diversification of exports. From the point of view of United States trade, our experience with Western Europe and Canada has long since shown that other industrialized countries make our best trading partners. If we see an equal need for agricultural modernization, both in greatly increasing productivity and in improving distribution, it is because agriculture has lagged behind industrial growth, causing serious economic and social pressures. We feel that both sectors must move forward together.

Another curious myth holds that United States support for monetary stabilization efforts in Latin America is intended to serve some selfish North American interest. But the sufferers from chronic inflation are not foreigners; they are the people of Latin America itself. We have supported monetary stabilization simply because reasonable price stability is a necessary foundation for effective development. Chronic inflation discourages savings, undermines social and political stability, diverts investment into wasteful uses, and makes it impossible to employ effectively the developmental resources we are making available in support of economic and social progress.

Then there are the myths concerning profits remitted abroad by private foreign investors, which have been so much discussed in Brazil. After hearing references to these profits as "suction pumps draining the Brazilian economy" I have taken the trouble to review the facts once again. The facts, taken from the figures of the Board of Currency and Credit (SUMOC), are that profits remitted to all foreign countries from Brazil have averaged 40 million dollars per year since 1947 and only 28 million dollars per year during the last five years. For each Brazilian, this amounts each year to 40 United States cents—more or less 150 cruzeiros at present exchange rates. So far as United States investors are concerned, they have regularly reinvested in Brazil a larger proportion of their earnings than they have remitted home.

Brazil has received in return, over the last fourteen years, foreign investment of risk capital of 1.3 billion dollars, and in the last five years over 700 million dollars. On the basis of the national accounts data of the Getúlio Vargas Foundation, total foreign loans and investments, private and public, have amounted to about one ninth of the total increase in Brazil's fixed capital during the last five years.

Without dominating the Brazilian scene, foreign capital—both in public and private loans and in risk capital —has played a vital part in the great development of recent years. Its direct contribution is significant enough, but it has had even more important results in stimulating the growth of Brazilian enterprise, both in partnerships and in purely Brazilian companies.

Again one thinks of São Paulo, center of a great Brazilian automotive industry which was created in four short years, with its 140,000 employees, 15 billion cruzeiros paid in direct taxes in 1960, and 1,300 companies producing automotive components. Most of these component firms are entirely owned by Brazilian shareholders.

Not only in automobiles, but in electrical equipment, pharmaceuticals, and the broadest variety of consumer goods, Brazil has been enabled through foreign investment to produce essential goods within the country, creating jobs for Brazilians, new working skills for Brazilians, taxes for Brazilian local, state, and national governments, and goods for Brazilian consumption incorporating the results of hundreds of millions of dollars worth of research and development expenditures undertaken in the more industrialized countries. At the same time, making these goods in Brazil instead of importing them from abroad has freed foreign-exchange earnings for the procurement of machinery and equipment and raw materials to continue the process of development and modernization.

There can be no doubt that Latin America faces a period of great challenge and great promise. Population growth and popular aspirations will not permit any mere cleaving to the *status quo*. The physical and human resources exist with which to build communities of growing material prosperity, of social justice, of ever greater opportunities for the coming generations, of respect for the human spirit, and of independent cooperation for peace and freedom in the world.

This has been the objective of all the great American Revolutions—revolutions which combined the French inspiration of liberty, equality, and fraternity with capacity for self-government and respect for divine law.

This is the message of *Mater et Magistra*. Development through tyranny and slavery is not the wave of the future; it is the wave of the past, seeking to engulf this Hemisphere as other reactionary waves of the past have sought without success. The true wave of the future is found in economic and social progress through the cooperation of free peoples. This is the meaning of Operation Alliance.

In this great undertaking which Brazil helped to inspire, Brazil not only can come to grips with her own pressing social and economic problems; she can become a model and a source of strength for other developing countries of this and of other continents. Brazil has already taught the world much. It is Brazil which ended slavery peacefully by the stroke of a pen and has achieved a degree of racial harmony which is the envy of other multiracial communities the world over. The Brazil which unified half a continent with a single language and under a single flag need not be humble about her capacity for achievement. And São Paulo is a living demonstration of the "Order and Progress" inscribed on the Brazilian flag.

3

ECONOMIC ASPECTS
OF THE ALLIANCE

* * * * * * * * * * * * * *

Although over half of my active life has been spent in public service, mainly on international affairs, as a result of the circumstances of the mid-twentieth century, I still regard myself as only an amateur diplomat. My true profession is university teaching. The Alliance for Progress is a topic that combines the most important single aspect of my work as United States Ambassador and my major field of professional concern as an economist during the last several years. Like many others in the United States, I have come to feel that policies and problems of economic development are the area within our discipline which most requires cultivation and understanding, not merely as an academic study but to provide objective analysis and competent technical guidance to the makers of policy.

The politicians will be seeking to promote development because there is an insistent popular demand for it. The economists have an important role in helping them to achieve real results, and at times in making clear to them the necessity for choice which the scarcity of resources imposes, and the costs and benefits involved in alternative choices.

It is something of a paradox that the systematic study of economics began two centuries ago with problems of development, but that they have only recently found their way back to the center of the stage. Development was the central concern of Adam Smith's "Inquiry into the Nature and Causes of the Wealth of Nations" and of the French physiocrats. Then, after many decades of preoccupation with distribution of income, marginal analysis, and micro-economics, the discipline has again turned to the most important issues of policy, including, first, problems of high employment and the trade cycle in the industrialized nations, and more recently problems of economic growth, with special emphasis on the less developed countries. It is a healthy sign, moreover, that many contemporary economists are dealing with this important subject not as "pure economics" (whatever that may mean), but as the combined economic, social, and political problem which it is in the real world.

I have previously tried to define the essential purpose of the Alliance for Progress in a few words, as follows: "A sustained and cooperative effort to accelerate economic growth and social progress throughout Latin

America, working through democratic institutions based on respect for the individual." Now I want to look more closely at the economic aspects of this program.

The Charter of Punta del Este, in its Title I, sets broad goals in terms of over-all economic growth; more equitable distribution of national income; balance and diversification of economic structures; accelerated industrialization; improved agricultural productivity and output; agrarian reform; broader and modernized provision for education, public health, and low-cost housing; price stability; Latin American economic integration; and improved stability of foreign-exchange earning. To promote more rapid growth, the Charter emphasizes the need for comprehensive and well-conceived national development programs. Long-term national plans had also been stressed in President Kennedy's original statement of March 13, 1961, proposing the Alliance for Progress. He said: "For if our alliance is to succeed, each Latin nation must formulate long-range plans for its own development—plans which establish targets and priorities, ensure monetary stability, establish the machinery for vital social change, stimulate private activity and initiative, and provide for a maximum national effort. These plans will be the foundation of our development effort and the basis for the allocation of outside resources."

Pending the preparation of national development programs, the Charter specifies a series of immediate and short-term action measures, including outside financial support for projects ready for implementation whose importance is so evident that they would obviously fit into any sensible long-term program. This transitional phase will necessarily vary in duration from country to country. I should like here, however, to review the concept of long-term national plans and the reasons for such great emphasis on this concept in the broad framework of the Alliance for Progress.

In the appendix to Title II of the Charter there appears an eight-point description of the essential elements of long-term national development programs. They are, in brief: (1) establishment of mutually consistent targets in the main economic and social sectors; (2) assignment of priorities and estimation of costs and benefits of specific major projects; (3) measures to direct the public sector and to encourage private action in support of the program; (4) cost estimates for the program in domestic currency and foreign exchange; (5) a calculation of internal resources available for development; (6) analysis of the balance of payments and of the necessary external financing; (7) the basic fiscal and monetary policies required to fulfill the program within a framework of price stability; and (8) the machinery of public administration, including measures for the cooperation of private organizations, to make the program effective.

Each national government is left free to determine the degree of detail to be used in its national program-making and is of course responsible for the selection of its own priorities. These are only in part technical matters; they also involve a wide range of choices on which every democratic nation will have its own scale of political preferences.

This concept of development programming must not be confused with the total planning of all aspects of economic life in the manner which is attempted in some totalitarian societies. It focuses on the major fields of public investment and on certain critical sectors of private (or mixed private and public) investment, especially those which can be bottlenecks in the development process or can be leading sectors for the economy as a whole. The main fields for programming typically include power, transportation, communications, education, housing, steel, cement, basic foodstuffs, major export commodities, and other selected industries, depending on the individual national structure. For the rest of the economy, such a national plan seeks to provide a framework conducive to general growth, by encouraging private competitive enterprise and the supply of adequate resources for long-term investment and for working capital within a framework of reasonable price stability.

The foundations for this sort of programming have been laid in Brazil during the last decade, notably in the Programa de Metas (Program of Targets). There are, however, two important ways in which the work done thus far falls short of the concepts in the Charter of Punta del Este. First, public investment in the social sector, although mentioned in the Programa de Metas, was not worked out in any detail. Secondly, there was no systematic effort to prepare two broad types of analysis indispensable to a general national development program: (1) a quantitative appraisal of the source and application of investment funds (i.e., a savings-investment account), and (2) a systematic appraisal of the balance of payments with assurance of external financing for any investment deficit.

Moreover, although sectoral planning and the establishment of priorities were quite thorough in certain fields, notably electric power and road transportation, there was only a limited effort to ensure mutual consistency among the various sectoral targets, and some were put forward only in very general terms.

Obviously economic development can take place without national programming. North America, Western Europe, Australia, and New Zealand have all achieved high living standards without going through this process. The Alliance for Progress, however, rests on the assumption that such planning, if well done, can speed up the improvement in economic and social conditions for which Latin American peoples are understandably impatient.

It is an evident fact that the supply of capital in Latin America is inadequate in relation to both needs and opportunities. Even with large-scale outside assistance, this will remain the case. The wastage of public investment resources on projects of low priority, or the reduction in productivity of capital resulting from unnecessary imbalances and bottlenecks in development, especially in such fields as power and transport with their wide economic repercussions, simply cannot be afforded. Moreover, over-all programming has the great advantage of imposing the discipline of choice—of appraising the total supply of domestic savings and foreign investment resources and considering consciously how that supply may best be used. It helps to make clear that the speeding up of some investments requires the slowing down or abandonment of others, or alternatively finding ways and means to expand the supply of capital.

A curious myth appears to have found some adherents in Brazil, to the effect that budgetary deficits are not inflationary as long as the amounts in deficit are used for productive investment. If this were so, there would be no limit to the supply of funds for public investment. Obviously real investments have to be financed by real savings, whether those savings are collected through taxation, through voluntary loans, or through the forced saving imposed on fixed income groups by inflation.

Over-all national programming should have the further advantage of demonstrating clearly the need for expanding voluntary saving, which is a good deal lower in Latin America than national income levels appear to make possible. There are wide opportunities for improving the structure of capital markets, the incentives and mechanisms for small savings, and the arrangements for financing of low-cost housing, all of which could greatly assist in mobilizing resources for developmental purposes.

I should like to make a special comment on the question of planning for investment in the social sectors. In the Charter of Punta del Este, as in the Act of Bogotá of 1960, emphasis is placed on four types of social investment: namely education, public health, housing, and improvement in rural living conditions. Systematic programming in these fields, with the possible exception of housing, is technically difficult. Education and public health do not return revenues directly to the investment, and the estimation of the economic benefits to the nation as a whole is still more of an art than a science, resting on very weak statistical evidence. Nonetheless, these types of investment in human capital may be not only desirable in themselves but also extremely productive economically. Preliminary studies in the United States of the economics of education show remarkably high rates of return, quite apart from the direct benefits of education in improving the human capacity to lead a good life. In the words of Professor Theodore Schultz of the University of Chicago, one of our wisest North American economists, human capital "is in substantial part a product of deliberate investment . . . it has grown in Western societies at a much faster rate than conventional (non-human) capital and . . . its growth may well be the most distinctive feature of the economic system."*

Although professional economists have made great

* Theodore W. Schultz, "Investment in Human Capital," *American Economic Review*, March 1961, p. 1.

progress in recent decades in developing systematic data for the macro-economic study of national economies, it is a misfortune that expenditures on education and health are treated as consumption rather than investment. This error will not be remedied overnight, and certainly not in time for the preparation of national programs under the Alliance for Progress. The very least that can be done, however, is to work out the basic data for sectoral plans in these obviously critical fields, so that choices can be made among them and the competing conventional investments.

In the field of education, for example, is there not a clear need for systematic national inventories of the present state of primary education, the cost involved in meeting the Alliance goal of six years' schooling for each child, the requirements for specialized manpower at the secondary and higher levels, the corresponding requirements for school construction, for teacher training, and for expansion and maintenance of the educational system?

In the agricultural field, should not a similar inventory be made of the requirements for an effective system of extension, credit, provision of seeds, tools, and fertilizers, and mechanisms for marketing and distribution? Without this, there is little hope for a successful attack on one of the most urgent aspects of development in Latin America—the achievement of higher agricultural output along with a radical improvement of living and working conditions on the land.

Such studies would provide a basis for realistic decisions of policy on how rapidly the goals could be achieved, on the necessary institutional reforms to achieve them, and on the choices between these and other developmental objectives.

Among the various sectors of social development, housing occupies a special category. In the conventional system of national accounts, housing is classified as investment rather than consumption, although in fact it is durable consumption rather than being productive in the same sense as investment in power, industry, agriculture, or education. Some economists have criticized the Act of Bogotá and the Charter of Punta del Este for giving too much emphasis to housing, basing their criticism on the ground that capital is scarce and cannot be afforded for this consumption-type purpose. Yet there is a burning and fully understandable desire for the improvement of housing conditions, which are not only generally inadequate for a minimum of human comfort and decency, but which also lead to widespread social discontent, especially in crowded city slums.

Here I would suggest that the professional economists may again be mistaken, although for a different reason. Our systems of national accounting are deceptively simple. They assume that total national output at any given time is fixed, that (except for the use of unemployed resources) it can be increased only by further investment, and that in the short run this fixed total output must be divided between consumption on the one hand and saving for investment on the other. But let us be wary of being fooled by our own magic. Let us always remember that our models, useful as they are, are only grossly oversimplified representations of the real world.

In that real world, even apart from the unemployed resources which are recognized in the conventional economic analysis, experience demonstrates that, with the right motivations, short-run output can be considerably increased without additional investment. If institutional machinery can be established for aided self-help housing projects, in which most of the labor is contributed by families which will own the houses, and if institutions to encourage small savings can be developed with home ownership as their goal, there is ample experience to suggest that extra labor will be forthcoming and extra savings will be forthcoming, greatly reducing the burden on other sectors of the economy. The Inter-American Development Bank is working with housing specialists from all of Latin America and from the United States, in an effort to create precisely such mechanisms and institutions, which are sorely lacking in most of the Hemisphere.

You will note that the major emphasis on detailed sectoral planning within the framework I have described above is on public investment in both the economic and social fields, together with a limited number of key areas of private investment where special forms of incentive may be desirable. For the remainder of the private sector, which in practice accounts for the bulk of total investment, a national plan would usually deal only in broad magnitudes, designed to ensure that sufficient resources of investment funds and of foreign exchange are available for healthy growth.

But if capital is scarce, it may be asked, is it not as important to avoid wastage of capital in the private sector as in the public? Should not the whole economy be planned in order to avoid such wastage? In my judgment, the answer to this question is clearly "no," for two reasons.

First, the planning organizations do not have, and cannot obtain, either the necessary information or the necessary wisdom to make correct judgments on the tens or hundreds of thousands of decisions which are involved.

Secondly, the dynamics of a market system, given a healthy environment for private enterprise and reasonably competitive conditions, will do this job infinitely better than any centralized bureaucracy could possibly do it. I have followed with great interest the path-breaking conceptual developments in economics of my Harvard colleague, Wassily Leontief, in his system of input-output analysis. These new intellectual inventions are of great importance for sound economic planning. But I have also noted the almost insuperable difficulties in estimating technical coefficients for a great variety of products and especially in forecasting what these coefficients will be a few years hence in a period of rapid technological change.

Market demand is not a static phenomenon, and the

means for meeting that demand are likewise not static. In a healthy system of private enterprise, there will be constant efforts to experiment with new areas of demand and with new methods of satisfying consumer needs, the market itself rewarding the efficient, squeezing out the inefficient, and guiding the flow of capital. In this process, one singularly important element, which distinguishes the private from the public sectors, is what I have called "the divine right to fail."

For much of the economy, therefore, it would be a wasteful misallocation of talent and resources to try to establish a centralized mechanism, aided by batteries of electronic computers, trying to solve thousands of simultaneous equations with dubious coefficients being fed into machines, in a stumbling effort to do through centralized decision-making what even an imperfect market mechanism does far better through decentralized decisions and widely dispersed initiative motivated by the search for profit.

There is another aspect of national planning in the Alliance for Progress which deserves special comment, namely the relationship between plans and practical operations. The files of government offices all over the world are crammed with paper exercises in national economic planning which bear no relationship whatever to actual results. Experience in dozens of developing countries has demonstrated that isolated planning commissions, whose work is not directly tied to national budgets, finance ministries, and the operating agencies which actually carry out public investments, are of little practical value.

Moreover, general plans are of little use unless they are built upon detailed sectoral plans, and above all on genuine and realistic planning of individual projects. It is for this reason that the Charter of Punta del Este refers to the need to justify specific development projects in terms of their relative costs and benefits. The engineering has to be well done, and the engineers and applied economists should be working hand in hand. Indeed, where trained manpower is scarce, more rapid results will be achieved by concentrating on effective project development than by the elaborating of ever more complex general plans.

Responsible officials of the World Bank have repeatedly told me that, in their present stage of operations, the supply of funds for projects for basic economic infrastructure is less of a bottleneck than the availability of competently prepared projects. This is not because underdeveloped regions are lacking in needs for transportation, power, and communications, but because they lack the engineering and economic skills to prepare projects with competence.

Thus far I have discussed mainly the Latin American side of the Alliance for Progress—the concepts of development programming, emphasis on the social sectors, the role of private enterprise within the framework of a development plan, and the relation between general programs and operational projects. But the Alliance is, of course, a cooperative effort, and the supply of outside financial and technical resources in sufficient volume and on suitable terms is a vital part of the whole.

The Charter of Punta del Este envisages a supply of capital from all external sources during the ten-year period of at least 20 billion dollars, much the larger part in public funds. Public funds from the United States alone will account for well over one billion dollars a year, the remainder being expected from international institutions, other friendly industrialized nations, and expanded private investment. The United States public share will approximate what was devoted in 1948–1952 to the Marshall Plan for European recovery, and the total from all sources will be substantially larger than the Marshall Plan.

What comes from outside, however, is meant to supplement Latin American efforts and not to substitute for them. The whole structure of the Alliance is based on the principle of self-help complemented by outside assistance. What is meant by "self-help"? In my view, three types of action are worth noting, all of them essential to a successful outcome.

First, on each individual project where outside resources are supplied, it is important that there be a substantial contribution of domestic resources as well. Without such a contribution, the place of the project in the Latin American national scale of priorities would be in doubt, and it would be difficult to look forward with assurance to effective maintenance and operation in the future. This type of self-help is essential to a true partnership.

Secondly, in many cases institutional improvements are required to make a particular project or program effective. These may be administrative arrangements—for example for the efficient operation of a water supply system or to establish agricultural or housing cooperatives. Or they may involve new legislation at the national or local levels.

Thirdly, there are the broader reforms which provide the framework for democratic progress. Securing reasonable monetary stabilization may be one of the most important of such reforms. Our recognition that large-scale inflation impedes balanced growth has led my government to provide very substantial financial help for the efforts of the Brazilian government to contain and reduce the rate of inflation. The reform of tax structures is another major example. Provision of equitable land tenure—necessary alike for long-run improvements in agricultural productivity and for social and political justice—is still another. Further examples could be cited, such as the modernization of educational structures and the fostering of smoothly working capital markets.

Let me make clear, however, that the Alliance in no sense contemplates a trading of aid in return for reforms. Meaningful reforms in democratic nations can only come from inside. They cannot be imposed or purchased from outside. The outside aid is conditioned on self-help only in the sense that without self-help in all three senses I have described, the basic purposes of the cooperative effort would fail. Self-help and outside support, therefore, must go hand in hand.

As compared with total economic activity in Latin America, even the large sums of outside assistance I have mentioned may seem small. They amount to something like 4 or 5 percent of the gross national product of Latin America as a whole. Let me remind you, however, that in the case of European recovery as well, assistance under the Marshall Plan in its first and biggest year likewise amounted to only 5 percent of gross European production. The critical importance of these outside sums arises from two fundamental economic points.

First, the outside resources all constitute additions, directly or indirectly, to the domestic resources available for investment. In relation to total investment funds, the ratio of outside support is nearer 20 or 25 percent than 4 or 5 percent. Beyond this, since the first charges on investment funds are the maintenance of the existing stock of capital and its expansion to keep up with population growth (which in the Brazilian case may alone require 10 percent of the gross national product), the assistance from outside becomes a very large share indeed of the vital increment of investment required to augment production and incomes per capita.

Secondly, the outside help relieves the pressure on the balance of payments, which is bound to be a serious limitation on growth in countries that are in a phase of rapid development and industrialization. There is a widespread view among Latin American economists that the terms of trade are constantly more unfavorable to countries whose exports are mainly in primary products. I am not satisfied that this view is adequately supported either by historical evidence or by theoretical considerations. Be that as it may, the importance of stabilizing markets for the major primary products is a recognized goal of the Alliance for Progress. In the especially important case of coffee, the new World Coffee Agreement shows real promise of success, despite the very great technical and political difficulties.

Apart from the question of changes in the terms of trade (and most arguments on this issue start by picking an abnormal base year for statistical comparisons), a developing nation in full course of modernizing its economic structure must inevitably require large-scale imports of capital goods for a period of at least some decades. In the Brazilian case, this problem is aggravated by deficiencies in domestic fuel and food resources. There is good reason to hope that both of these deficiencies can be greatly reduced during the coming decade. For the present, however, outside aid which combines the supply of capital with the supply of foreign exchange is substantially more valuable than an equivalent volume of additional domestic capital formation.

Apart from these quantitative points, foreign aid has qualitative advantages because of the technology it brings with it. I would emphasize, in this connection, not only methods of production and other scientific and engineering knowledge, but equally important methods of organization and administration which are an essential part of economic modernization.

The private-investment component of the outside support under the Alliance for Progress has an especially important role to fulfill in this respect. Its contribution to the supply of capital is itself substantial, but its contribution to the modernization of methods of production, distribution, and industrial and agricultural management may in the long run prove even more valuable. Wherever possible, I should like to see foreign private investment take the form of joint ventures with Latin American capital. This not only would reinforce the principle of partnership already emphasized but would also assist in the more rapid diffusion of modern techniques. In most fields of agriculture, mining, and manufacturing, no other method for the rapid transfer of such techniques is remotely as effective as private international investment.

There has been considerable confusion about the relation of private investment to the balance of payments. One type of calculation commonly made seems to me simply bad economics. This is to count as a gain to the balance of payments the import of capital, and to count as a loss the repatriation of capital together with remitted profits. All of these items should properly be taken into account. But sight must not be lost of the very great effect which the product of the investment may have on the balance of payments through replacement of imports or expansion of exports.

In recent years, so long as foreign investors have been equitably treated, most of them have not only shown no disposition to repatriate capital, but have continually augmented capital through new investments and through the reinvestment of a good share of their profits. As a result, the net effects of foreign private investment have been highly favorable to the balance of payments of developing countries. This is so much the case that some commentators in the United States, concerned with our own large balance-of-payments deficits in recent years, have given serious attention to the idea of limiting investment abroad. Fortunately, responsible authorities are not disposed to entertain this idea, at least with respect to the less developed regions of the world.

There should be no effort to hide the fact that the goals of the Alliance for Progress pose a high challenge for all of our governments and for responsible leaders from all of our peoples. The Alliance rests on a cardinal element of faith, the faith that personal dignity and political liberty are supreme values and that free peoples can find ways of pressing forward with economic and social progress through free institutions. The human and material resources of Latin America, supplemented by the outside assistance which is now being made available, are fully capable of overcoming the technical obstacles to progress, provided that political energies and leadership are dedicated to that objective.

4

DEVELOPMENT AND THE
DEMOCRATIC REVOLUTION

* * * * * * * * * * * * *

"This Alliance is established on the basic principle that free men working together through the institution of representative democracy can best satisfy man's aspirations, including those for work, home and land, health and schools."

The representatives of twenty nations at Punta del Este, making this statement in their Declaration to the Peoples of America, were not only restating a fundamental value of Western civilization—that the State is to be the servant, and not the master of the people. They were also asserting their confidence that free institutions have the capacity to devise the mechanisms to combine economic progress with social justice and to discharge these tasks both effiicently and responsibly.

This capacity is not self-evident to all. I was asked in

a press conference in Goiânia whether it was really credible that such misery as exists in certain areas of Brazilian life could be remedied through democratic means. I replied that both history and logic demonstrate that the answer is "yes." Democratic means do indeed have that capacity, and they are the only acceptable means for people who possess and who value their freedom.

The twenty nations' expression of confidence in representative democracy sets a high standard for leadership, not only in the political sphere but in private business, in trade unions, in agricultural cooperatives, in universities, and in the many other organized associations which are moving forces in free societies. In the public sector, it means standards of integrity, impartiality, and efficiency rather than the favoritism and jobbery which still occupy too large a part of the political scene, and not only in Latin America. In the private sector, it means acceptance of social responsibility by business concerns in dealings with employees and consumers, and by trade unions in promoting the cause of justice for the working class. It means cooperation among all elements in the community to expand productivity rather than a self-defeating effort to equalize poverty. And it means responsible control of political leadership by an electorate informed by a free and honest press.

Not all of these high standards will be achieved overnight. I know of no democratic society where they have been fully achieved, although I would be happy to face a fair comparison between democracy and totalitarian regimes in all these respects.

Whatever its faults, democracy possesses two cardinal virtues, which I dare say are the reasons that Winston Churchill has described it as "the least bad form of government." It does not permit the State to enslave the people. And it ensures an effort to move constantly forward from the *status quo*, always seeking—even if never entirely reaching—the ideals which Abraham Lincoln had in mind in speaking of government "of the people, by the people, for the people."

I was once asked—not by an entirely friendly questioner—whether the underlying idea of the Alliance for Progress was "to maintain the *status quo* of the democracies in Latin America." The more I reflect on this question, the more peculiar it seems. True democracy never means maintenance of the *status quo* in Latin America, in the United States, or anywhere else in the world. True democracy cannot mean maintenance of the *status quo*, since it makes political power responsive to the popular desire for change. True democracy, in short, is the regime of continuous social revolution.

In many parts of the world, representative democracy has proved its efficiency as a means of social revolution. I use the word *revolution* to mean a process of structural change in society—an alteration in the pattern of social classes, in the social mobility of individuals and their children, in the educational structure, in methods of production, standards of living, and the distribution of income, and in attitudes toward relationships among individuals, business and other private organizations, and the State.

The fact that the democratic revolution is generally nonviolent does not make it any less revolutionary. Nor is it an easy process. There are always vested interests opposed to social change, and some of them can be toughly resistant. Our own history contains a classic example of the failure of democratic processes to contain the stresses generated by an historically inevitable restructuring of our society and economy. As a result, a long, bloody, and costly civil war had to be fought to hold the nation together. But it is also clear that the nonviolent revolutions are normally more durable than the violent. A century later, the bitterness of our civil war still haunts our race relations. The Brazilian emancipation from slavery came later but more peacefully, and it has yielded results in interracial harmony which are the envy of the world and from which we in the United States can learn much.

If one surveys the modern history of Western Europe, one sees representative democracy gradually transforming the whole character of the British nation from a society dominated by feudal landowners into a modern industrialized welfare state which is now clearly of and for the people. And one sees greater social change in the last two generations of working democracy in France than in the two generations of the famous violent French Revolution, with its aftermath of terror, reaction, and restoration.

The fact is that representative democracy has, built into it, powerful pressures for social change, because those entrusted temporarily with the power of government are compelled to be responsive to persistent aspirations of large and dissatisfied elements in the community. And the successive major changes then come to be part of the consensus accepted by the entire community. The reforms involved in our own New Deal, for example, which were resisted with much bitterness a generation ago, are now accepted as common ground.

In all this process of social and economic change, however, certain basic moral and political values have been held constant. The moral values are those of Christian civilization and respect for the dignity of the individual human being. The political values are those of government with the consent of the governed. This does not mean the mere appearance of consent, manufactured by a state monopoly of press and radio and by mob rallies masquerading as spontaneous demonstrations of the people. It means true consent, expressed through representative institutions, including the secret ballot, with effective freedom of press, assembly, and political party organization.

No thoughtful person in the so-called "advanced industrial nations" of Western Europe or North America regards the process of development and social change as complete. The essence of the democratic revolution is that it is never finished. We in the United States recognize the deficiencies in the still-existent slums of many of our large cities, in our race relations, in the continuing need to strengthen our educational structure, in the social and economic effects of automation and other technological development, in the overproduction of certain agricultural products, and in many other fields. But we remain confident that through democratic institutions these and other social problems yet unidentified can be analyzed and overcome.

If one examines objectively the economic systems which operate today in North America and Western Europe, one sees a remarkable degree of similarity among them and a remarkable degree of consensus within each nation on their basic validity. Communist propaganda tries to persuade us that these are all "capitalist systems," obeying the inexorable laws of decay of Marx's historical determinism. If one uses the word "capitalism" simply to mean an economic system in which agricultural, industrial, commercial, and financial activities are carried on mainly by privately owned companies and private individuals, then these are indeed capitalist systems. But consider the framework in which private enterprise works in these countries.

First, the ownership of the enterprises, instead of being confined to a small moneyed class, is becoming increasingly diffused in many hands. Among the owners are now found a large number of stockholders from the middle and working classes, often including the employees of the companies themselves, and the large pension funds that have been built up by the trade unions.

Second, the task of management has become increasingly separated from ownership and entrusted to a growing professionalized corps of trained administrators. This "managerial revolution" has had an important effect on the attitudes and policies of private companies.

Third, while in many industries technological considerations require large-scale units, monopolies are forbidden outside the public-service sector (where they are regulated), and there is keen competition among the various companies for shares of the market, for research and development of new products, and for improved methods of management to reduce costs.

Fourth, wages and working conditions are determined, not by the simple will of the employers, but through collective bargaining with highly organized free trade unions.

Alongside the privately owned companies, the system includes an important network of cooperatives, especially producers' cooperatives in the agricultural field and also many consumers' cooperatives. In the agricultural sector, there are special governmental incentives and aids to production—sometimes perhaps too effective—but all supporting a system of farms owned by the farmers themselves.

As to the role of government in economic life, there

is a significant range of enterprises under direct governmental management. More important, there is a complex framework of guidance, influence, and control which greatly influences private business policies.

Government policy, moreover, reflects a resolution of many forces. Businessmen are one important force, as indeed they should be, since they are directly responsible for the operation of much of the nation's economic life. But business interests are by no means monolithic and united. Labor organizations have substantial political influence, also not always monolithic and united. Farm organizations, professional groups of every variety, civil servants, and even university professors and other intellectuals all have a voice in the process of persuasion and debate that ends with governmental policy determination. And national political leadership has a major role in shaping and guiding the entire process.

In short, these governmental systems of the industrialized nations of the free world are pluralistic systems, greatly affected by what my Harvard colleague and our Ambassador to India, Kenneth Galbraith, has called "the concept of countervailing power."* In truth, this economic system can scarcely be called simple "capitalism"; it must at least be called "neo-capitalism" or "democratic capitalism" or "a democratic enterprise system" or perhaps simply a "mixed economy."

* John Kenneth Galbraith, *American Capitalism: The Concept of Countervailing Power* (Boston: Houghton Mifflin, 1952; revised edition, 1956).

It is significant that in Western Europe, the democratic socialist parties have been moving away in recent years from their sponsorship of the traditional socialist principle of public ownership of the means of production as an end in itself. They have learned that the mere transfer of enterprises to governmental hands guarantees neither efficient operation nor social justice. On the contrary, it often carries with it inefficiency, jobbery, and the political abuse of economic power. The European socialist parties have therefore come to favor other, indirect means of fostering the interests of the working classes they represent. They have found that a system of dispersed control and initiative through private ownership and economic management, coupled with indirect governmental incentives and restraints, is a more productive form of economic organization which can be completely harmonized with the objectives of social equity.

If the idea of "socialism" means social justice and responsiveness to the interests of the broad masses of the people, then these neo-capitalist democratic mixed economies are much more "socialist" than the Communist systems which have appropriated the term. In truth, the Communist regimes have as little right to call themselves "socialist" as they have to apply the term "democratic" to the completely totalitarian, one-party dictatorships of the Eastern European satellite countries.

Let us compare these democratic mixed economies with the predictions of Marx and Lenin concerning what they called the inevitable evolution of capitalism. I will cite only four outstanding examples to demonstrate the hollowness of this pseudo-science.

First, Marx predicted that the capitalist system would be characterized by widening class differences and ever more intensive class warfare. The workers could never obtain more than minimum subsistence wages. What has happened? A century later, the workers of these mixed-economy countries are full participants in the fruits of economic progress and are indeed the best customers of the industries in which they work. Social class distinctions are tending to disappear entirely. If Marx's predictions had been correct, it would hardly be the announced goal of the Communist countries to "catch up" with the living standards of these downtrodden and exploited North American toiling masses with "nothing to lose but their chains." Speaking personally, I hope that they do catch up—and not only with the living standards but also with the respect for divine law and human liberty which are the more important superiorities of the West. And they should, since Russia and Eastern Europe are legitimate partners in the great heritage of Western civilization.

Second, Marx and Lenin foresaw a series of increasingly severe business cycles and financial crises in the capitalist world. The neo-capitalist world has now gone thirty years without unmanageable financial disruptions, and there is every reason to believe that Western economic science and policy have ruled out for good anything like the disastrous depression of the 1930's.

Third, based on the lack of internal markets resulting from the subsistence wages of the proletariat under capitalism, Lenin foresaw a series of bloody struggles among the capitalist nations in their effort to conquer outside markets through imperialism. For a while in the latter nineteenth century, especially during the partition of Africa, this prediction seemed to have some substance. But how does it stand up today? With only a few rapidly disappearing remnants of European imperialism, Western Europe is enjoying a dramatic new surge of growth. The most prosperous Western nations are those which never had colonies or which lost them early, such as the United States, Canada, Australia, Switzerland, Sweden, and West Germany. And while Western Europe has been freeing its colonies rapidly in these postwar years, and abandoning its chauvinistic nationalism in favor of regional integration, the Communist system has been conquering and holding new colonies through the use of undisguised force.

Finally, the Marxist doctrine holds that "bourgeois democracy" is only a pretense, and that governments are simply committees of management on behalf of the capitalist ruling classes. It is amusing to look at this doctrine through the eyes, let us say, of a twentieth-century Swede or Norwegian or Dane or Dutchman. For anyone with even a nodding acquaintance with American history, it is not precisely easy to think of Theodore Roosevelt, or Woodrow Wilson, or Franklin Roosevelt as "tools of Wall Street." Nor has President Kennedy appeared to be a slavish instrument of the steel industry.

In short, the forces of representative democracy, impelled by the popular drive for social change, have proved much stronger than Marx's so-called historical inevitability.

Someone may say that this is all well and good for the presently industrialized countries, which have had favorable natural environments and which entered the industrial revolution many decades ago. But are there reasons for confidence that the democratic revolution can work similar miracles in Latin America? To answer this requires some analysis of the process of economic growth.

Without endorsing every detail, let me call attention to the extremely stimulating study by Professor Walt Rostow of the Massachusetts Institute of Technology, now head of the Policy Planning Staff of the Department of State.*

Professor Rostow, basing his theory on a careful study of the actual process of development in many countries of the world during the last three centuries, sees five major stages in the growth process. They are: (1) the traditional societies, not unlike the old plantation agricultural arrangements of colonial South America; (2) the "preconditions for takeoff," a transitional process providing a foundation for the great agricultural and industrial revolutions; (3) the "takeoff into sustained growth,"

* W. W. Rostow, *The Stages of Economic Growth: A Non-Communist Manifesto* (London: Cambridge University Press, 1960).

which Rostow calls the "great watershed in the life of modern societies"; (4) the "drive to maturity," a phase normally extending some sixty years after the beginning of the "takeoff"; and (5) the "age of high mass consumption," a stage still limited to the industrialized countries of North America, Western Europe, and Australasia.

I have tried to classify the situation in Brazil in terms of this theory, and I can only conclude that Brazil is in at least all of the four first stages simultaneously, depending on the region which is being observed. The State of São Paulo, considered by itself, is clearly well on the way from "takeoff" to maturity. Certain other regions are not far behind. São Paulo still has many problems, but if all Brazil were at the economic level already reached by São Paulo, and developing with the speed with which São Paulo continues to develop, would there be any doubt whatever as to Brazil's national capacity to assure a bright economic and social future?

This does not for a moment mean that São Paulo and the other more advanced areas of Brazil do not still require outside capital. On the contrary, Rostow's analysis shows that the period between "takeoff" and economic maturity is precisely the phase in which nations have the greatest absorptive capacity for imported capital and can make the most productive use of it. Foreign public and private investment has entered the State of São Paulo on a large scale in the years since the war. The economy has benefited greatly from it. I hope that this flow will continue for many years to come, and that it will be intensified through full participation in the Alliance for Progress.

In the less-advanced regions, however, such as the Brazilian Northeast, the problems of accelerated development are more difficult and substantially different in character. But similar situations have been effectively dealt with by democratic means in such cases as Southern Italy, our own Tennessee Valley, and the island of Puerto Rico. In all these cases there have been three keys to genuine progress.

The first key is an intensive and well-planned program of public investment to supply both the economic and the social infrastructure (such as roads, power, water, education, and public health) required for rapid development. Though industrial development has an important part to play, the main thrust must be toward improvement in agricultural productivity and better distribution of agricultural income, since agriculture will inevitably be the principal occupation in such regions for a very long period. And I emphasize social investment along with the economic, because without improvement in human capital—especially in health, educational training, and agricultural extension services—the provision of roads, power, and water can not achieve their full potential.

The second key is special incentives to attract private investment, in order to get over the hump of initially low returns which create a vicious circle of stagnation. There are many types of such incentives. Tax concessions, market guarantees, government assistance in providing plant sites, technical assistance, and credit on unusually favorable terms have all proved their usefulness.

The third and perhaps most important key is full economic integration with the wealthier regions of the nation. If the development of a depressed region were tackled in isolation, this would add immeasurably to the difficulties. Such a region must look to the wealthier areas for markets for its own specialized products, for supplies of capital goods and other goods which can be made more cheaply in the advanced areas, and for the furnishing of financial capital and technical assistance which will be attracted by the special incentives previously referred to. Southern Italy is finding this to be true in its relations with Northern Italy, and Italy as a whole in its relations with the rest of the European Common Market. A most hopeful sign in this connection is that businessmen in São Paulo are giving serious thought to investment in Brazil's Northeast. The economic progress of the Northeast will clearly benefit São Paulo by providing a major addition to the domestic market.

An agreement has been signed committing the United States to large-scale assistance to supplement the Brazilian government's program for accelerated development in the Northeast. The joint financing under this agreement fits within the framework of the three key lines of policy I have mentioned. The Brazilian Northeast is recognized by all concerned as one of the greatest challenges in Latin America to the declarations of policy set forth in the Charter of Punta del Este.

On the national as well as the regional level, the Alliance for Progress requires for its success an effective process of over-all programming for economic and social development; the selection of priorities; the preparation of sound specific investment projects; the promotion of basic reforms in taxation, in education, in the agrarian structure, and in other institutions required to assure a wide distribution of the benefits of development; and the principle of national self-help supplemented by prompt and effective external financial and technical assistance.

As I hope I have made clear by now, my faith that democratic institutions are fully capable of making good the intentions stated at Punta del Este does not mean at all that I suppose this success will be automatic or easy. We all know that democracy has its weaknesses as well as its strengths. We know the ease with which persuasion can degenerate into demagogy and policy can degenerate into politicking. We know the temptations to jobbery and corruption—although democracy has no monopoly on those evils. We know the example of the legislator (in a country that had better be nameless) who boasted that he had never voted against an expenditure, and never voted in favor of a tax measure, and had always been re-elected. We know that administrative reform has a very high priority along with reforms in education, taxation, and land tenure.

Protection against these weaknesses is a task for enlightened political leadership and for enlightened public opinion. A free democracy does have the resources to assure that such abuses will not remain hidden and has the means to correct them if the will exists.

5

REBUILDING THE
EDUCATIONAL FOUNDATIONS

* * * * * * * * * * * * *

Economic development and social progress, as I have said, are Siamese twins, and social development, properly conceived of as social investment, is itself a major factor in the process of economic development. This is the case with public health, which improves the productive capacity of the people. It is the case with improved agricultural living conditions. But it is especially true with education, which if properly designed can prove and has proven to be a more productive form of investment than any of the conventional economic investments in physical works.

In education and training, no less than in physical investment, lies the secret of relatively high economic development in nations poor in natural resources, nations such as Switzerland and Israel. If one examines the miracle which Japan performed in the second half of the nineteenth century, converting itself in a few decades from a tradition-bound feudal society into a modern industrial nation, it is clear that the introduction of universal education played a critical part. In the United States, recent evidence suggests that perhaps one half of the fourfold increase in our per capita incomes during the last seventy-five years is due to the improvement in human capital through education and training, the other half coming from science and technology and from investment in physical capital.

In Latin America, of all the underlying conditions which keep living standards today so far below the levels that the human and material resources of the Hemisphere make possible, none is more important than the deficiencies in educational structure. Those deficiencies are universally recognized. They are both quantitative and qualitative. No basic reform could do more to accelerate the much-desired processes of economic and social progress than the broadening and modernization of this educational structure.

From the human and social viewpoint, this reform is essential to realize the human potentials which are often simply lost through the absence of any available schooling or through the gross deficiency in educational opportunities beyond the rudiments of primary school. From the economic standpoint, a modern society needs specialized skills at all levels, from highly trained university engineers, agronomists, physicians, scientists, administrators, accountants, and economists, down through the intermediate ranks of agricultural and mechanical technicians, and skilled office workers.

Developing countries, in their struggle to close the gap with more highly industrialized communities, have many disadvantages and obstacles to overcome, but they also have one great advantage. This is the opportunity to learn from the experience of others, to borrow and adapt the methods of production, distribution, and organization that others have found through decades of slow experimentation and development. I emphasize adaptation rather than copying, since the methods must be adjusted to the special conditions and desires of each developing country. In an age of increasing technological complexity, this process of adaptation simply cannot be accomplished without a modern educational system.

It was for these reasons that the Charter of Punta del Este included as one of its explicit goals for the coming decade the following: "To eliminate adult illiteracy and by 1970 to assure, as a minimum, access to six years of primary education for each school-age child in Latin America; to modernize and expand vocational, technical, secondary and higher educational and training facilities, to strengthen the capacity for basic and applied research; and to provide the competent personnel required in rapidly-growing societies."

In March 1962 there took place in Santiago de Chile a major international conference on education and its relation to economic and social development in Latin America. There the goals of Punta del Este were further reviewed against the background of such systematic information as could be gathered with the help of national ministries of education and all the international agencies concerned. The background papers for this conference make it clear that there exists a woeful deficiency in the basic information required for effective educational planning; but the tentative data available show that Latin American countries as a whole devote only 2 percent of their gross national product to education. To reach the minimum goals, even after allowing for improvements in the efficiency of educational methods, this proportion should be doubled to 4 percent by 1970, and should be supplemented by substantial external resources, which the Santiago meeting estimated at some 150 million dollars a year. The representative of the United States made clear our readiness to cooperate with effective Latin American programs for educational expansion and modernization.

Looking at some of the information developed for that conference concerning Brazil, in relation to other Latin American countries, we can see that a number of major points stand out. There are major deficiencies in meeting Brazil's legal standard of four years' universal primary education, deficiencies especially marked in the Brazilian North and Northeast, and in rural areas of the country generally. (Parenthetically I might note that the legal standard in most of Latin America refers to a minimum of six years rather than four, but these higher

targets are not necessarily matched by higher performance.) There is the sudden and sharp shrinkage of the
educational stream between the primary and the secondary levels, much more severe in the case of Brazil than
in the other large Latin American countries. Within the
secondary school system, there is an acute shortage of
technical and vocational training, both rural and urban.
So it is clear that if the needs of a rapidly developing
economy are to be met, there is not only a very large
task ahead in the completion of the primary school system, but relatively an even greater need for expansion
and modernization of intermediate and secondary educational training. Finally, at the higher level, there are
problems not only of numbers but even more of remedy-
ing qualitative weaknesses, especially in such fields as
engineering, agriculture, and administration.

It is sometimes asked whether Latin America can af-
ford universal education. I would point to two persuasive
reasons for believing that it can. When my own state of
Massachusetts introduced the first system of free, com-
pulsory, universal education in the world, at the very
beginning of the nineteenth century, our then stage of
economic development was far behind what exists today
in Brazil and in several other Latin American nations.
If experience elsewhere is canvassed, it will be found
that certain nations in Asia and Africa, also substantially
poorer than Latin America, are now beginning to provide primary education for all of their children.

To serve its purposes, however, the educational system must be designed to meet the needs of the developing society. Two centuries ago, one of our early educational philosophers made a somewhat oversimple distinction between "useful" and "ornamental" education. Primary education is clearly a foundation for both. At the secondary and higher levels, however, the distinction takes on more validity. I have a clear impression that the broad design of Latin American educational systems, modeled largely on the late nineteenth-century experience of continental Europe, does not adequately serve the "useful" side of present-day needs. In societies seeking rapid industrialization and higher agricultural productivity and modernization of their structures of production and distribution, there is a vast requirement for technical and vocational education at the secondary level, and for engineering, medicine, economics, and administration at the higher level.

I do not argue that Latin American education should be a carbon copy of our own system, although I firmly believe that our experience, for example, with agricultural colleges, and with university training in engineering and administration, contains many lessons of value for the other American republics. I would also point out that the European educational structures are themselves being modernized in the directions I have just suggested.

But it is clear that the best kind of "useful" education also carries with it a large component of the "ornamental," since leadership in the professions and in all sectors of organized private and public life calls for minds that are not only disciplined but also cultivated and reflective. The conference at Santiago de Chile, like all conferences on education, did not fail to pay its respects to the classic question of humanistic versus materialistic education. Having myself been raised in the humanistic tradition, but having observed carefully the process of vocational and professional education at the higher levels, I should like to emphasize my firm conviction that this is largely a false dilemma. Though it is possible for vocational and professional training to be narrowly materialistic, the best forms of such training are aimed at making not only good specialists, but good citizens and truly cultured human beings.

The qualities of mind that are called for certainly include the basic disciplines of language and number, the rigorous logic of mathematics and the physical sciences, the respect for hard fact and for objective evaluation of events. But they also include an understanding of the varieties of human experience and the complexities of the human spirit; its emotions and passions as well as its capacity to reason; and the creativity which distinguishes men from beasts. History, philosophy, literature, poetry, music, and the other arts all have some part in such an education. It is clear, moreover, that formal education—whether at the primary, the secondary, or the higher level—must equip the student for the continuing process of education in the course of his adult life. Training in the capacity for further learning is at least as important as the actual learning of the school years themselves.

It is significant in this connection that our great land grant colleges, originally founded exclusively for training in the agricultural and mechanic arts, and our own great technological institutes, such as the Massachusetts and California Institutes of Technology, have now evolved into fully rounded universities in the broadest meaning of that term. The myth that the American educational system is devoid of humanistic elements is largely a product of Western European writers whose only acquaintance with the United States comes from motion pictures. This myth is happily being dispelled by the greater volume of first-hand contacts.

I would not expect educational reform at the higher level in Latin America to follow slavishly any single pattern elsewhere in the world. Latin America has a wide variety of models to study and will doubtless evolve its own patterns, especially adapted to its own needs and circumstances. In considering the relation between education and economic development, however, I would point out that our own system of land grant universities, one hundred years old in 1962, is the foundation for the most highly productive system of agriculture in the world. There are now sixty-eight such universities, accounting for about one fifth of the total higher education in the United States. They include research centers of the highest quality. Their work is directly linked to the national government's system of agricultural extension services. Now these do not claim to be perfect institutions. Year by year they are themselves modifying their curricula and methods, since like all dynamic organizations they have long recognized the need for self-criticism. But they certainly have a great deal of value to offer to a continent with a crying need for higher agricultural output and for improved living conditions on the land.

This immense challenge of rebuilding the educational foundations of Latin America is directly related to two other types of institutional change: tax reform and administrative reform.

To double the proportion of total national income devoted to education obviously requires drawing on new sources of tax revenue and distributing the resulting receipts appropriately among the various levels of government responsible for different sectors of the educational process. In cases where a large budgetary deficit is already a major source of inflationary pressures, the need for tax reform is all the greater.

But it is equally clear that the educational effort can succeed only with a substantial improvement of the administrative structure. It requires systematic planning, the proper relating of teacher training to school construction, and the use of educational methods that will give the greatest results per unit of expenditure. This in turn requires a body of properly paid, properly trained, and genuinely professional civil servants for educational administration. And trained administrators are also indispensable in other sectors of government activity and private business.

One of the most striking aspects of the revolution in private enterprise which has developed during the past half century—starting in the United States and then spreading to the other industrialized nations of the free world—has been the development of professional management. It is trained not only in the applied sciences of engineering and production and the applied economics of finance and accounting, but also in the more complex applied social science of human relations—the organization of effective working groups through the free consent and active participation of their component members. And it is trained in the concepts of responsibility, not only to shareholders in the enterprise, but also to the consuming public, the local community, and the broader national and world communities whose well-being is essential to the health of the enterprise itself.

The training of such managers for both public and private administration, and at both the secondary and the higher levels, is itself one of the great needs to be fulfilled by the educational structure.

In the field of education, then, we see exemplified all of the basic principles of the Alliance for Progress—the principles of systematic planning, self-help and institutional reform, and timely and effective outside technical and financial help. Clearly the education sector cannot be developed in isolation from the rest of the national economic and social development. On the demand side, the need for trained people depends on the pace and character of the development taking place in other sectors. And on the side of supply, the resources to be devoted to education must be properly weighed against the needs for transportation and power, agriculture and industry, housing and public health.

The building of a structure of modern education may not appear as dramatic as other types of basic reform which have been so widely discussed in connection with Latin American economic and social progress. But experience the world over has repeatedly and unequivocally demonstrated that social reform is not merely a matter of legislation. To achieve real results, it requires the building of institutions with people and training and organization.

Nor should the speed with which educational reform produces measurable results in economic and social terms be underestimated. Educational reform was a key to the astounding transformation of Japanese society. In the last fifteen years, it has been a key to the remarkable contrast between the living standards of Israel and those of her neighboring Arab countries in the Middle East. It has been a key in the development of modern industry and technology in the Soviet Union. In a young country like Brazil, with almost half the population below the age of fifteen, education can produce major results with extraordinary rapidity.

Broadening the educational base is also vital to the

democratizing of the social structure. True democracy not only means political rights for all; it also means genuine equality of opportunity with an open road for people of talent however humble their social origins. If half the children of school age fail to have schooling, what an appalling waste of potential human resources for a nation! Educational opportunity is the key to mobility of social classes and therefore to lasting and constructive social change.

6

FREE INITIATIVE AND
THE ALLIANCE FOR PROGRESS

* * * * * * * * * * * * * *

Despite all the well-known problems of inflation, of regional and sectoral imbalances, of lags in education and agriculture and housing, and of administrative deficiencies, the Brazilian economy has continued to grow rapidly. This foundation of things already accomplished inspires confidence that further and better-balanced development can go forward, and that the problems and deficiencies, if courageously and realistically faced, can be overcome. But obviously Brazil needs rapid further economic and social development. It is a country of very rich potential, but with living standards for most of the population far below the levels which could be achieved. Of course people are not satisfied with their present living standards and want better ones for themselves and their children.

Furthermore, with the population increasing at the rate of two and one quarter million per year, new jobs must be found at the rate of one million a year. And I mean genuinely productive jobs, not fictitious "make work." The investment and economic expansion required simply to provide these jobs, in addition to raising average living standards, is substantial. It is a striking fact that, although the population of the United States is two and one half times that of Brazil today, the population is increasing so much more rapidly in Brazil that the annual task of additional job creation is almost the same size in the two countries. But with total production in Brazil today only one twentieth that of the United States, it can readily be seen how formidable a task Brazil faces in achieving the necessary pace of economic expansion.

As Brazilian businessmen well know, economic development is not achieved by waving some magic wand. To establish or expand an individual business requires hard effort to plan the enterprise, to mobilize resources for investment, to organize and train the work force, to assemble the machinery and equipment, to develop the supplies of water and power and raw materials, the networks of distribution and marketing, and the financial and accounting controls to ensure that the business is being run at a profit. National development is the sum of many thousands of such individual developments.

It is the purpose of the Alliance for Progress, as it was of the original Brazilian proposal for Operation Pan America, to speed up national development through a combined process of effective national planning, institutional reforms, and complementary large-scale assistance from other friendly nations, all within a framework of free institutions and democratic liberties.

Some commentators have apparently been led to suppose that, because of the emphasis of the Act of Bogotá and the Charter of Punta del Este on social progress, the Alliance for Progress is merely a program of social welfare. This is not the case. It is true that the Alliance emphasizes social progress along with economic development, and that it expects national development plans to include provision for education, health, improved rural living conditions, and low-cost housing. It also stresses the special problems of backward regions such as the Brazilian Northeast, which have not shared sufficiently in the progress of recent decades. But the basic philosophy is to promote rapid economic development in order to increase total production—the total availability of goods and services—simultaneously providing for their more equitable distribution and for full participation in progress by all segments of the population. Without much greater total output, mere redistribution of incomes would simply mean distributing poverty.

At the same time, the Alliance recognizes that certain forms of so-called social investment, notably in public health and education, are important not only for their immediate contribution to social welfare, but also because they are indispensable elements in economic development. They are indeed among the most productive forms of investment which a society can make.

Where does private enterprise fit into the philosophy of the Alliance for Progress? A careful reading of the Charter of Punta del Este shows that private enterprise has a role of primary importance. It is the main source of initiative and of action in the development of industry, agriculture, finance, commerce, and distribution. A major purpose of the over-all developmental planning so strongly emphasized by the Charter is to provide a framework of institutions and incentives to encourage the most rapid possible expansion of constructive private enterprise and to ensure that an adequate share of the total resources for investment will be available for use by the private sector.

This form of planning for development does not mean centralized control of the whole economic structure on totalitarian lines. It means planning that is concentrated on two essential elements: (1) an integrated program of public investment in economic and social infrastructure for which government has direct responsibility, with assured financing on a non-inflationary basis, and (2) provision of a framework of institutions and incentives within which private enterprise can function efficiently. The government development plans, in a sense, may be likened to the arteries of a healthy human being, with private enterprise providing the blood cells which flow through those arteries.

Obviously each nation must make its own decisions as to the range of economic operations it wishes to be managed directly by the government. It should be noted, however, that it is not easy to organize efficient public administration even for the minimum functions which any modern government undertakes. On the social side, there is the huge task of modernizing the educational system, including the provision of universal primary education, technical and vocational secondary education, and higher education redesigned to meet the needs for specialized manpower for rapid progress. Systems of public health, social security, and agricultural extension services are additional major governmental tasks whose successful organization is essential to rapid modernization. On the economic side, there are the basic networks of transportation, communications, and supply of power and water, in all of which government operation and government financing necessarily play a large part.

How far a nation wishes to go beyond this in operating certain basic industries depends partly on the availability of private resources for these purposes and partly on political considerations which each community must evaluate for itself.

From the point of view of efficient development, the important requirement is that such public enterprises be well operated—technically, administratively, and economically. And it would be simply blindness not to recognize that there are certain built-in obstacles, which are not easy to overcome. There is the problem of avoiding political criteria in the selection of personnel. There is the problem of avoiding excessive centralization of what are essentially business-type decisions. And there is the problem of applying objective accounting standards to costs and expenditures to avoid hidden subsidies really made at the expense of the people themselves.

In nations with a long tradition of highly efficient public administration, such as England, Switzerland, and Germany, these obstacles are largely overcome by organizing government enterprises on a true business basis, completely insulated from politics. In other countries, the experiences generally have been less successful. It is significant that Socialist political parties in the free countries of Western Europe have in recent years tended to abandon state operation of industry as a political goal, finding that private operations within a framework of governmental regulation which encourages competition and ensures fair treatment of labor and consumers are better guarantors of high productivity and of social justice than are the outmoded theories of state socialization. And as to agriculture, surely even the more doctrinaire Communists must be harboring doubts about collective and communal farms which provide neither adequate production nor even political satisfaction for the peasants.

In seeking to speed up development, a modern government must undertake, along with a well-conceived program of public investment, the even harder task of providing a healthy economic framework. First and foremost is the need for a system of money and credit to meet the needs of a modernizing economy without substantial monetary inflation. In the highly industrialized countries, there is much discussion as to whether monetary policies should aim for complete stability or should welcome a gentle inflation of perhaps 1 to 5 percent per year. But I know of no one who believes that economic development is helped by inflation on the scale experienced since the war in Bolivia or Chile—or since 1959 in Brazil. Such inflation reduces the total volume of savings required for development and distorts the patterns of investment, pushing much of it into nonproductive channels. It is a source of continuing social and political unrest arising from the struggle of every segment of the society to protect its relative position as the money continually depreciates. In particular, it weakens the middle class whose growth is indispensable to real economic and social progress.

Nor is there any secret about the sources of such inflation. It results from large governmental deficits financed by the printing press and from an unbridled expansion of credit without regard to genuine economic expansion in real terms.

Severe inflation undermines the whole system of financial institutions, inevitably leading to enormous interest rates to compensate for monetary depreciation, and to all sorts of devices for evading the legal ceiling on interest charges. In order to put some real content back into the financial world, it even leads to a curious new monetary unit, "multiples of the minimum wage," already adopted for certain criminal penalties. And it always contains the danger of getting completely out of hand, degenerating into a spiral of galloping inflation and perhaps even to a totally worthless currency, as occurred in Germany in 1923.

Apart from money and credit, a sound governmental framework for promoting development would include encouragement of a smoothly working capital market, stimulating both small and large savings, and means to channel them into the most productive forms of investment.

But if private enterprise is to play its full part in this great challenge of rapid development, there is also a need for modernization within the private sector itself. This is the special responsibility of the business leader.

If one surveys the evolution of business in North America and Western Europe over the last fifty years, one sees a complete transformation in attitudes, organization, and methods of operation.

The old view was that a business existed solely in the interests of its owners, and that they could best pursue that interest by squeezing the most out of their consumers through a monopolistic policy of low output and high prices, and by squeezing out their competitors through every device of jungle warfare, legal or illegal.

The modern view asserts that business is an organization for a social purpose, whose markets depend on ever-increasing real wages for the lower and middle classes of the nation; that the businessman is a professional manager with responsibilities not only to shareholders but also to consumers, workers, and the society at large; and that open competition within an expanding economic environment gives far better results—even from the narrowest viewpoint of profit and loss statements—than restrictive monopolies. This modern view places a high priority on ever-increasing productivity, achieved through better organization and administration, technical modernization, and labor relations which secure the willing cooperation of the work force in reducing costs and expanding output.

In nations like France and Italy, this sea change in business attitudes has largely taken place during the last fifteen years, in the course of postwar recovery with the help of the Marshall Plan and in the subsequent development of the European Common Market. Organized productivity centers have played a large role. The old idea of each business seeking a protected position, bolstered by various legal privileges and zealously guarding business secrets from competitors, charging consumers high prices for small volume, and battling its own employees as if they were enemy No. 1, has given way to open competition for shares of a constantly growing market, cooperation with labor in improving productivity, and concentration on scientific and technical advance to meet new consumer wants.

And what is the result? In place of economies that have been stagnating for decades, there is one of the highest rates of economic growth to be found anywhere in the world. The larger national output is being more widely and justly distributed to the benefit of all concerned.

I see no reason whatever why similar methods and similar attitudes should not bring even more fruitful results in Latin America, where the opportunities for expansion and development are so much greater than in the densely populated old continent.

In this connection, I am repeatedly surprised by a widespread attitude to be found in Latin America concerning business profits. There seems to be a feeling that profit is ugly, antisocial, and something that businessmen should be ashamed of. It is true that there are certain types of purely speculative profit, or monopoly profit, which deserve this criticism. But in a healthy and competitive economic system, profits are a sign that the business enterprise is meeting real consumer wants, keeping its costs below the prices that consumers are willing to pay. This is a sign of real service to the economy, which should be a source of pride and not of shame. The businessman who should be ashamed is the one who makes losses, since he is either not meeting consumer wants or does not do as efficient a job as his competitor.

If the criticism is directed against monopolistic profits, the target should be not the profits but the monopolies. In that field, the experience of the more industrialized free countries shows workable approaches to an effective antimonopoly or antitrust policy which can ensure healthy competition without going to the extremes of cutthroat competition. This is another important institutional improvement for modernizing societies bent on constructive development.

What should be the role of foreign private enterprise in the process of Latin American economic development? The importance of this role has recently been set forth in clear terms by the joint Senate and Chamber committee of the Brazilian Congress, prepared by Senator Mem de Sá. That report makes clear the contribution of foreign private investment not only to the total capital supply in Brazil over the last fifteen years, but also to the modernization of Brazilian industry through the introduction of new techniques and more productive methods of organization and management. It also stresses the great contribution made by foreign investors to the creation of jobs, the expansion of the national product, and the availability of tax revenues at all levels of government.

In this connection, the American Chamber of Commerce in São Paulo recently assembled data on twenty-four large North American industrial investors in Brazil, which include the following striking figures for the year 1961. At the end of that year they were giving employment to over 61,000 persons, practically all Brazilians. During the year they paid wages and pensions of 19 billion cruzeiros. They contributed over 100 million cruzeiros to charitable, educational, and professional associations. And their tax payments to national, state, and local governments amounted to 20.5 billion cruzeiros. This seems to me to show a very large contribution to the growth and welfare of the Brazilian economy.

In December 1961, I visited the automobile show in São Paulo, and more recently the heavy industry show there. No one can see such displays of industrialization in Brazil without being enormously impressed. I am told that some representatives of the Soviet exposition also visited the heavy industry show, and remarked at the end that they would now have to revise their ideas about the state of Brazil's economic development. I am not surprised. I imagine that they had heard so much from their agents and friends about Brazil's need for economic emancipation that they supposed that Brazilian industry was still in the middle ages.

In this connection, perhaps I should also report the observations of some Brazilians who visited the Soviet exposition in Rio. They said that, except for the exhibit on outer space, the quality of the merchandise there made it clear that Mr. Khrushchev should establish a new economic target for the Soviet Union: "Catch up with Brazil!"

Now most of the individual companies represented in the expositions in São Paulo are owned entirely or in large part by Brazilian shareholders. Yet almost all of them had benefited from technical and managerial developments pioneered in the United States, Germany, France, Japan, or other free industrialized nations. And it was through the channel of direct investment by foreign enterprises, often working in partnership with Brazilians, that these great advances were made in Brazilian development.

When remarks are made about foreign investment "sacking" the Brazilian economy, one cannot help observing that it is the State of São Paulo which has shown the greatest surge forward in recent years, the greatest improvements in real wages, tax revenues, and general economic growth, and it is also in the State of São Paulo that the vast bulk of foreign private investment has been concentrated during this period. The obvious conclusion would appear to be that foreign investment not only should not be repulsed, but should be eagerly sought.

I have sometimes heard it said that Latin American competitors of foreign firms are concerned that the large resources of the foreign parent companies for research and development place competing Latin American business at an inevitable disadvantage. It is evident that resources are available in the United States and in Europe and Japan for research and development on a scale very much larger than Brazil or any other Latin American country can hope to undertake for many years to come. But is the answer to this problem to exclude the foreign developments in science and technology? I should have thought precisely the reverse. One of the great advantages of the developing countries is their ability to borrow from and use the techniques pioneered by others at great expense. This is, indeed, one of the reasons for expecting much more rapid development in Latin America in the twentieth century than took place in the nineteenth century elsewhere. It is the most promising way of closing the gap between Latin American and North American living standards. To shut out the advanced technology, in order to preserve vested Latin American interests in less efficient methods of production, would be simply a prescription for permanent impoverishment.

Paradoxically, at the same time that some voices in Latin America are heard denouncing foreign investment, the already far more advanced Western European countries are vigorously competing to attract foreign investment from one another and from the United States and Japan. They offer special inducements and incentives and undertake a concerted program of information and publicity on the advantages of investing in their countries.

This type of policy does not result from any special fondness for, or influence by, North American business. It results, rather, from a clear recognition of the true national self-interest of the Western European countries. It is the economic counterpart of that enlightened contemporary political wisdom of Western Europe which has turned its back on the demagogic nationalism which placed the peoples of Italy and Germany under the heels of Fascist tyrants and which twice in this century brought Western civilization to the verge of total destruction. That new policy looks to the *interdependence* of freely cooperating free nations as the true wave of the future.

Speaking on July 4, 1962, the 186th anniversary of our national independence, President Kennedy declared that the United States will be ready for a declaration of interdependence with this rapidly uniting Europe—a mutually beneficial partnership which, in his words, "would serve as a nucleus for the eventual union of all free men—those who are now free and those who vow someday to be free." He made it clear that under modern world conditions we in the United States can no longer, acting on our own, attain our basic goals of peace, freedom, prosperity, and social justice. But if we act in voluntary partnership with other free nations, there is every reason to hope that these goals can be secured, not only for us but for all.

Why should Latin America not be the third foundation stone in this great international enterprise for peace, freedom, prosperity, and social justice? It will be said that economic and social conditions do not yet make this possible. Very well, then. This obstacle can be overcome in a decade of intensive development through the Alliance for Progress, so that the whole of this New World can play its full part in making a better world for mankind at large.

7

PRODUCTIVE TENSIONS
IN THE DEVELOPMENT
OF THE WESTERN HEMISPHERE

* * * * * * * * * * * * *

I feel a certain uneasiness about any implications that we should be seeking the abolition of all tensions. The opposite of *tension* is *relaxation*. Suppose that there were a "Conference on Relaxation in the Development of the Western Hemisphere." What a horrid thought! The fact is, of course, that tensions can be either constructive or destructive. Psychologists tell us that all life is an alternation between tension and relaxation. War involves disagreeable tensions. Love involves highly agreeable tensions. And work involves necessary tensions. Professor Albert O. Hirschman, in his classic book on the strategy of economic development,* has shown how unbalanced economic development, which many econo-

* Albert O. Hirschman, *The Strategy of Economic Development* (New Haven: Yale University Press, 1958).

mists consider purely wasteful and which certainly does create tensions, can be a most powerful spur to growth, provided that the leading sectors are of the type which drag along the others more rapidly than they would move in the course of non-tensional, vegetative, relaxed development.

I suppose, therefore, that our task is not to look for ways to avoid or eliminate tensions in the development of the Western Hemisphere, but rather to stimulate the productive tensions and to dissipate the obstructive. And my present purpose is to offer some thoughts on both productive and frustrating tensions in making a reality of the promise of the Alliance for Progress and the Charter of Punta del Este.

It is well to remind ourselves that the Charter of Punta del Este, agreed upon in August 1961, states at the outset of Title I: "It is the purpose of the Alliance for Progress to enlist the full energies of the peoples and governments of the American republics in a great cooperative effort to accelerate the economic and social development of the participating countries of Latin America, so that they may achieve maximum levels of well-being, with equal opportunities for all, in democratic societies adapted to their own needs and desires." The Charter then specifies goals of economic and social progress and ways and means for achieving those goals. These include national programs of coordinated public investment and stimu-lated private investment, special attention to social progress, institutional reforms and improvements, action to improve Latin American trading conditions, and systematic support through external technical and financial assistance. In the last paragraph of the Declaration to the Peoples of America, which was adopted simultaneously with the Charter, there is reference to a new era for the inter-American community, supplementing its institutional, legal, cultural, and social accomplishments "with immediate and concrete actions to secure a better life, under freedom and democracy, for the present and future generations."

How does all this look a year later? Candor compels us to recognize that it is a very mixed picture. On the technical side of developing programs and projects, a good deal has been done. The Inter-American Bank has played an indispensable part in speeding up this process. Some Latin American governments have greatly strengthened their administrative machinery for program-making and selection of priorities. On the side of the United States government much headway has been made in building a new organization and in gradually converting the working methods of bureaucracy to the new spirit called for by the Alliance for Progress. The lists of specific institutional reforms and improvements in Latin America make an impressive showing.

Yet it is clear that the "full energies of the peoples and governments" have not yet been enlisted in this effort. There is not yet a sense of a great cooperative effort as the highest priority of the inter-American community, securing the devoted efforts of the most talented leaders in public and private life throughout the Hemisphere. Democratic institutions remain under very great pressure, and in some cases they are once again temporarily in eclipse, although not irrecoverably.

Why these shortcomings? It would take a detailed country-by-country analysis to explain and account for all of them. In Brazil, political life has obviously been overshadowed by the crisis following the resignation of President Quadros soon after the Charter of Punta del Este was adopted. In my opinion, however, the basic shortcoming has been squarely identified by Roberto Campos, the Brazilian Ambassador to the United States, when he speaks of the need for a political mystique.

Unless the pursuit of economic and social progress, in the terms of the Charter of Punta del Este, becomes a major part of the national political life of each participating country, and unless the great majority of people and organized groups and leaders of influence feel themselves involved and committed to these goals, the Alliance for Progress will not succeed regardless of the technical soundness of individual projects and the amounts of foreign financial support made available to Latin America. The Alliance then will become simply another American aid program, no doubt larger and better than its predecessors, but not a cooperative process for bringing about a real sea change in the actual standards of living, in the prospects for their further rapid improvement, in the sense of participation in progress by all classes and regions of the national communities, and in the security of civil liberties and the institutions of representative democracy.

The underlying will for accelerated economic and social progress under free institutions clearly exists in Latin America. To be sure, there are minorities in opposition. There are vocal minorities on the far left, whose main interest is in overthrowing free institutions. They fight the idea of democratic progress just as the Communist parties in Western Europe fought the Marshall Plan fifteen years ago. There are less vocal, but powerful, minorities in the traditional oligarchies, and sometimes among the newly rich industrialists, who are too satisfied with things as they are to be receptive to any kind of change, even though experience elsewhere might suggest to them that they could find a useful, satisfying, and rewarding place in a progressive democratic society. But I would guess that taken together these minorities account for no more than 15 or 20 percent of the peoples of Latin America. The problem is to find and encourage articulate and effective leadership for the aspirations of the vast majority, and to relate a political mystique to the technical problems that must be objectively diagnosed and solved.

That sort of leadership clearly must be Latin American; it cannot come from outside. The supreme merit of ex-President Kubitschek's idea of Operation Pan America was precisely that. This Brazilian statesman conceived of a cooperative movement led by Latin American nations, and supported by the United States and other friendly countries, to make expanded economic development the central objective of organized public and private effort in this continent for this decade. I have always regretted that our own government did not fully recognize the potency of this idea when it was launched four years ago. It did win partial recognition in the decision to establish the Inter-American Development Bank and in the Act of Bogotá, and it won full recognition in the Charter of Punta del Este. Nevertheless, it has not yet developed the political drive which its success requires.

The Alliance for Progress is often compared to the Marshall Plan. The differences are greater than the similarities. Development is a far more difficult undertaking than economic recovery, and the administrative institutions of Latin America, as well as the economic and social infrastructure, are much less developed than were those of Europe in the late 1940's. But the European experience does contain some useful pointers.

At a certain point in the development of the Marshall Plan, there became evident a compelling need for European political leadership at a high level as part of the formal cooperative machinery. And when the idea of European integration was conceived as the basis for a great new move forward on the foundation of postwar recovery, it was given vital political leadership by Jean Monnet and his Action Committee for the United States of Europe, a necessary informal prerequisite to the later establishment of formal institutions for economic and political unification.

Nor were these movements limited to cabinet ministers and public officials. They sank their roots into the national communities, enlisting members of parliament, political parties, organizations of businessmen, labor unions, and the liberal professions, universities, the press, and other organs of mass communication. Is there not in this experience something to be drawn on for guidance in the contemporary Latin American scene?

The Charter of Punta del Este gives deliberate stress to the importance of immediate social investments, along with large-scale economic investments, and it also emphasizes institutional and structural reform. I believe that these emphases are sound. Social investments, properly conceived, are complementary to economic investments and are major elements in an effective development program. In addition, both social investment and structural reforms are essential to a full sense of participation in the development process by all elements of the population, and therefore essential to the national cohesion and sense of popular identification which the success of the Alliance for Progress requires.

But there is much misunderstanding on this point, certainly in Brazil. I often hear criticisms of the so-called *assistential* character of the Alliance, as if it were only a program for charitable palliatives of the misery which is so widespread in this continent. This is a gross mis-understanding. The term *assistential* may prehaps be applied to a campaign to eradicate malaria or to measures to eliminate the many debilitating diseases which come from impure water, but public health programs of this type are essential to an economically productive population as well as to a happier one. And education, which is conventionally considered to be social investment, has been proven to be one of the most economically rewarding forms of investment that any nation can make, providing that it is properly designed to meet the needs of a rapidly modernizing society.

The most acute problems of internal tension in carrying out the Alliance for Progress arise in connection with structural reforms. Agrarian and tax reforms are cited most frequently. Equally important, in my view, are reforms in the organization, working methods, and attitudes of public administration; reforms to modernize the administration of private business; educational reforms; and reforms in the financial institutions which stimulate savings and channel them into constructive investment. All these types of reform are indispensable to economic and social progress. Perhaps the Act of Bogotá and the Charter of Punta del Este can be given some credit for the fact that discussion of basic reforms has become a commonplace of Latin American politics. Every office-seeker must declare his devotion to such reforms, no less than to national patriotism and to motherhood. But, evidently, different users of the phrase have many different things in mind, and many users probably have nothing specific in mind at all.

Many discussions of the politics of reform seem to me to be oversimplified. It is often assumed that there is a one-dimensional political spectrum, running from revolutionary reformers on the far left, through a center of varying breadth composed of democratic reformers, and ending with reactionary anti-reformers on the far right. No doubt this spectrum exists, but it is certainly not the only political dimension.

Cutting across it, for example, are conflicting ideas on the nature of governmental institutions. There is one well-entrenched tradition of government as a patron of special interests, serving not only wealthy oligarchies, but also specially privileged labor unions, and furnishing innumerable useless jobs for protégés of various political parties. This contrasts with the concept of government as a body of efficient public administrators serving the broad public interest. There is another dimension which separates demagogues who prefer attractive but mean-ingless slogans (which may be of the left, right, or center) from political leaders who seek real remedies for the social and economic problems which cry for solution. And there is a further dimension which sepa-rates distributive reformers from expansionist reformers.

In any society where great wealth exists in the hands of a few, the idea of dividing their wealth among the many has an obvious popular appeal. Every civilization in recorded history shows examples. In societies with low average income, the contrast between poverty and wealth is especially marked, because the middle class is small and the wealthy few may be, like the old-time princes of India, wealthy to a degree wholly unknown in modern industrialized societies. No one could claim that such societies are socially just, and distributive measures obviously must play some part in their modernization. But where average standards are low, mere distributive measures add no significant real income to the masses. They add only the psychic income of seeing the once mighty laid low. If the desire is for genuine economic and social progress for the entire community, the main thrust of reforms must be directed toward development, growth, investment, and higher efficiency in production and distribution.

The reformist philosophy of the Charter of Punta del Este embraces both developmental and distributive objectives. In translating these principles into practice, obviously each nation will have to find its own patterns, suited to its geographical and social conditions and its popular aspirations. But unless the primary emphasis is placed on expansion, the wherewithal to meet those popular aspirations simply will not exist.

In this connection, the North American New Deal of a generation ago seems to me a highly instructive experience. The New Deal brought about major transformations in the structure and attitudes of United States society, most of which have long since been accepted by both political parties and all sectors of opinion despite their highly controversial character when first initiated. Reviewing the principal features of the New Deal, with the advantage of a generation's hindsight, one sees clearly that its great successes were those measures which looked toward economic expansion and growth, and the reshaping of institutions within a context of such growth. Its failures were the measures which reflected the gloomy view—quite widespread at the time and later wholly disproved by history—that the American economy was already overbuilt and that reforms must simply distribute what could be produced under a regime of perpetual stagnation.

The measures looking toward growth were able to create new harmonies among interest groups and classes which would have been condemned to civil warfare against one another within a context of stagnation. Let me mention a few examples. Regulation of the stock market was not designed to destroy Wall Street and the investment bankers; it was designed to reform the capital market, replacing speculation by true investment, and to open the way for democratization of stockholding in the large business corporations. The systems of housing and farm credit insurance were not designed to socialize the housing industry or agriculture; they were great social inventions in collaboration between government and private enterprise, which made possible the enormous postwar programs of rehousing and of higher agricultural productivity. The Tennessee Valley Authority was born of a refusal to accept the inevitability of backwardness in that underdeveloped region; it sought instead to promote balanced growth through efficient use of water and land resources and systematic community development. The social security system met the most pressing needs of old age and unemployment insurance, and added important stabilizing influences to the economy as a whole, but it could never have been afforded under conditions of economic stagnation. The public utility holding company law rebuilt the financial structure of the electrical supply industry, not by punishing or expropriating the operating companies, but by placing them on a firm foundation for future expansion and improved service.

The outstanding failure of the New Deal was the National Industrial Recovery Act. This measure sought to cartelize the economy, to spread limited working opportunities thin through reduced hours of work, and to spread limited market opportunities thin through monopolistic agreements to reduce production and maintain prices. It fortunately endured for only two years.

The New Deal contained many other faults, including a spirit of undiscriminating antagonism toward the business community at large. But it also had the great virtue of a political mystique. It asserted the self-confidence of the nation in its capacity to cope constructively with its economic and social problems. It expressed a passion to include fully in the national society certain formerly forgotten groups—the Negroes, the migratory farm workers, the marginal farmers of the South, and the urban workers not yet organized into trade unions. And it applied a highly pragmatic and realistic approach to specific problems of social engineering. All these elements seem to me very relevant indeed to the contemporary Latin American scene.

The need for realism in social engineering poses a special challenge to Latin American universities, which are another focus of internal tensions in the development of the Hemisphere. It is from their student ranks that leaders must come for the continuing struggle for economic and social progress.

During the last few decades, Latin American faculties of medicine and engineering have felt compelled to adopt truly professional standards, with rigorous training and strenuous devotion to studies by the student body. The reasons are evident. Without such training, the medical patients die and the bridges and buildings collapse. In many, perhaps most, parts of Latin America, however, the illusion remains that *social* engineering is still a matter for dilettantes—for part-time students of law and of economics taught by part-time professors. Young men can graduate with honors, persuaded that glibness in verbal expression is an adequate substitute for respect for hard facts and for rigorously objective thinking. They are encouraged to confuse the *ought* with the *is*, to believe that a social structure has been built when an aesthetically pleasing design has been drawn—or even an impressionistic sketch. But if effective development is to take place, the faculties of law and economics must develop the same toughness as the faculties of medicine and engineering. Without this, one can expect continued diseases in the body politic and continued collapses in the social structures.

Let me mention a few examples of this problem of realism in social engineering. In facing the problem of chronic inflation, the realists will look for the basic causes in budgetary imbalances, excessive credit expansion, wage increases without regard to productivity, and structural bottlenecks in critical areas of production. They will not be satisfied with emotional outbursts against convenient scapegoats such as foreign investors or greedy speculators.

In dealing with public utility services, the realists may choose either management by government or management by private enterprise, but they will insist on efficient management and on the service's paying its own way. They will recognize that when a telephone or power service is subsidized, that subsidy is not truly free. It is a gift to the fortunate users at the expense of generally poorer non-users, who pay the cost either through general taxes or through inflation. Such a policy not only contradicts economic sense; it violates the most elementary canons of social justice.

The realists, similarly, will be most interested in agrarian reform, but they will not be satisfied with mere promises to give land to the landless. They will insist on obtaining the facts as to how land is owned and used, and on devising patterns of productive use which will raise agricultural productivity and permit the earning of a decent living by farm families. They will combine reforms in land tenure with the organization of agricultural credit, supplies of seeds and machinery, and effective mechanisms for storage, marketing, and distribution.

Such an approach to social engineering will not dissolve all the tensions implicit in economic and social change. But it will give the constructive tensions the pre-eminence they deserve. Surely this is a challenge to enlist the passions and the intellectual energies of the university youth in Latin America who are rightly dissatisfied with things as they are. If they were to analyze coolly the human and material resources of this Hemisphere, they would see that the objective problems of social and economic development are far more readily soluble here than in the great underdeveloped continents of Asia and Africa. But they would also see that development cannot be achieved by waving magic wands, by exorcising foreign scapegoats, by drafting five-year plans without the necessary machinery to put them into effect, or by distributing poverty without creating new wealth. And they would see that steadfast cooperation among the Latin American nations can bring much greater results than isolated national efforts, and that the effective collaboration of friendly foreign nations can make a critical difference between success and failure in a limited period of time.

I said at the start that a political mystique is indispensable to the success of the Alliance for Progress, and that leadership in the creation of this political mystique must come from Latin America. I do not mean by this to suggest that we North Americans have no useful role to play. On the contrary, we have an indispensable role. We are the major source of outside technical and financial support, and it is no easy job to organize ourselves to supply that support promptly and effectively. We need to convey a much better understanding than now exists in Latin America of the nature of our own society and the reasons that impel us, perhaps somewhat belatedly, to join in this great cooperative partnership with Latin America. We must also dispel certain suspicions and doubts, some deliberately fostered by the Communists and their allies, but others which result from the historic tensions within the Hemisphere. There exists, for example, a concern that the Alliance for Progress might undermine the sovereignty and the independence of Latin American nations. I know that I speak for our government as well as for myself in saying that we do indeed believe in ultimate interdependence, rather than independence, but it is the interdependence of freely cooperating peoples and nations, each independently making its own decisions to work with the others in its own deepest interest.

It is also true that we in the United States have our own real national interest in the success of the Alliance for Progress. This is not a selfish interest, however, in the sense of being a gain for North America at the expense of Latin America. It is rather a national interest which converges with those of our Latin American neighbors. It is our interest that there be a Western Hemisphere of prosperous, self-reliant, and securely democratic nations. And if we look ahead, our imaginations cannot help but be inspired by the idea of a great triangular Western community in which Latin America, Western Europe, and North America are the firm foundation units for an ever-widening area of peace, of freedom, and of liberation of the human spirit in the world as a whole.

APPENDIX

TEXTS OF DOCUMENTS
APPROVED AUGUST 17, 1961,
AT PUNTA DEL ESTE, URUGUAY

* * * * * * * * * * * * *

Following are the Declaration to the
Peoples of America and the Charter of
Punta del Este, the two principal documents
establishing the Alliance for Progress.
They were approved by the representatives
of twenty American republics at a special
meeting of the Inter-American Economic and
Social Council at the Ministerial level.
The republics are: Argentina, Bolivia,
Brazil, Chile, Colombia, Costa Rica,
Dominican Republic, Ecuador, El Salvador,
Guatemala, Haiti, Honduras, Mexico,
Nicaragua, Panama, Paraguay, Peru,
United States, Uruguay, and Venezuela.

DECLARATION TO THE
PEOPLES OF AMERICA

* * * * * * * * * * * * *

Assembled in Punta del Este, inspired by the principles consecrated in the Charter of the Organization of American States, in Operation Pan America and in the Act of Bogotá, the representatives of the American Republics hereby agree to establish an Alliance for Progress: a vast effort to bring a better life to all the peoples of the Continent.

This Alliance is established on the basic principle that free men working through the institution of representative democracy can best satisfy man's aspirations, including those for work, home and land, health and schools. No system can guarantee true progress unless it affirms the dignity of the individual which is the foundation of our civilization.

Therefore the countries signing this declaration in the exercise of their sovereignty have agreed to work toward the following goals during the coming years:

To improve and strengthen democratic institutions through application of the principle of self-determination by the people.

To accelerate economic and social development, thus

rapidly bringing about a substantial and steady increase in the average income in order to narrow the gap between the standard of living in Latin American countries and that enjoyed in the industrialized countries.

To carry out urban and rural housing programs to provide decent homes for all our people.

To encourage, in accordance with the characteristics of each country, programs of comprehensive agrarian reform, leading to the effective transformation, where required, of unjust structures and systems of land tenure and use; with a view to replacing latifundia and dwarf holdings by an equitable system of property so that, supplemented by timely and adequate credit, technical assistance and improved marketing arrangements, the land will become for the man who works it the basis of his economic stability, the foundation of his increasing welfare, and the guarantee of his freedom and dignity.

To assure fair wages and satisfactory working conditions to all our workers; to establish effective systems of labor-management relations and procedures for consultation and cooperation among government authorities, employers' associations, and trade unions in the interests of social and economic development.

To wipe out illiteracy; to extend, as quickly as possible, the benefits of primary education to all Latin Americans; and to provide broader facilities, on a vast scale, for secondary and technical training and for higher education.

To press forward with programs of health and sanitation in order to prevent sickness, combat contagious disease, and strengthen our human potential.

To reform tax laws, demanding more from those who have most, to punish tax evasion severely, and to redistribute the national income in order to benefit those who are most in need, while, at the same time, promoting savings and investment and reinvestment of capital.

To maintain monetary and fiscal policies which, while avoiding the disastrous effects of inflation or deflation, will protect the purchasing power of the many, guarantee the greatest possible price stability, and form an adequate basis for economic development.

To stimulate private enterprise in order to encourage the development of Latin American countries at a rate which will help them to provide jobs for their growing populations, to eliminate unemployment, and to take their place among the modern industrialized nations of the world.

To find a quick and lasting solution to the grave problem created by excessive price fluctuations in the basic exports of Latin American countries on which their prosperity so heavily depends.

To accelerate the integration of Latin America so as to stimulate the economic and social development of the Continent. This process has already begun through the General Treaty of Economic Integration of Central America and, in other countries, through the Latin American Free Trade Association.

This declaration expresses the conviction of the nations of Latin America that these profound economic, social, and cultural changes can come about only through the self-help efforts of each country. Nonetheless, in order to achieve the goals which have been established with the necessary speed, domestic efforts must be reinforced by essential contributions of external assistance.

The United States, for its part, pledges its efforts to supply financial and technical cooperation in order to achieve the aims of the Alliance for Progress. To this end, the United States will provide a major part of the minimum of twenty billion dollars, principally in public funds, which Latin America will require over the next ten years from all external sources in order to supplement its own efforts.

The United States will provide from public funds, as an immediate contribution to the economic and social progress of Latin America, more than one billion dollars during the twelve months which began on March 13, 1961, when the Alliance for Progress was announced.

The United States intends to furnish development loans on a long-term basis, where appropriate running up to fifty years and in general at very low or zero rates of interest.

For their part, the countries of Latin America agree to devote a steadily increasing share of their own resources to economic and social development, and to make the reforms necessary to assure that all share fully in the fruits of the Alliance for Progress.

Further, as a contribution to the Alliance for Progress, each of the countries of Latin America will formulate a comprehensive and well-conceived national program for the development of its own economy.

Independent and highly qualified experts will be made available to Latin American countries in order to assist in formulating and examining national development plans.

Conscious of the overriding importance of this declaration, the signatory countries declare that the inter-American community is now beginning a new era when it will supplement its institutional, legal, cultural and social accomplishments with immediate and concrete actions to secure a better life, under freedom and democracy, for the present and future generations.

THE CHARTER OF
PUNTA DEL ESTE

ESTABLISHING
AN ALLIANCE FOR PROGRESS
WITHIN THE FRAMEWORK OF
OPERATION PAN AMERICA

*   *   *   *   *   *   *   *   *   *   *   *   *

PREAMBLE

We, the American Republics, hereby proclaim our decision to unite in a common effort to bring our people accelerated economic progress and broader social justice within the framework of personal dignity and political liberty.

Almost two hundred years ago we began in this Hemisphere the long struggle for freedom which now inspires people in all parts of the world. Today, in ancient lands, men moved to hope by the revolutions of our young nations search for liberty. Now we must give a new meaning to that revolutionary heritage. For America stands at a turning point in history. The men and women of our Hemisphere are reaching for the better life which today's skills have placed within their grasp. They are determined for themselves and their children to have decent and ever more abundant lives, to gain access to knowledge and equal opportunity for all, to end those conditions which benefit the few at the expense of the needs and dignity of the many. It is our inescapable task to fulfill these just desires—to demonstrate to the poor and forsaken of our countries, and of all lands, that the creative powers of free men hold the key to their progress and to the progress of future generations. And our certainty of ultimate success rests not alone on our faith in ourselves and in our nations but on the indomitable spirit of free man which has been the heritage of American civilization.

Inspired by these principles, and by the principles of Operation Pan America and the Act of Bogotá, the American Republics hereby resolve to adopt the following program of action to establish and carry forward an Alliance for Progress.

TITLE I. OBJECTIVES OF THE ALLIANCE FOR PROGRESS

It is the purpose of the Alliance for Progress to enlist the full energies of the peoples and governments of the American republics in a great cooperative effort to accelerate the economic and social development of the participating countries of Latin America, so that they may achieve maximum levels of well-being, with equal opportunities for all, in democratic societies adapted to their own needs and desires.

The American republics hereby agree to work toward the achievement of the following fundamental goals in the present decade:

1. To achieve in the participating Latin American countries a substantial and sustained growth of per capita income at a rate designed to attain, at the earliest possible date, levels of income capable of assuring self-sustaining development, and sufficient to make Latin American income levels con-

stantly larger in relation to the levels of the more industrialized nations. In this way the gap between the living standards of Latin America and those of the more developed countries can be narrowed. Similarly, presently existing differences in income levels among the Latin American countries will be reduced by accelerating the development of the relatively less developed countries and granting them maximum priority in the distribution of resources and in international cooperation in general. In evaluating the degree of relative development, account will be taken not only of average levels of real income and gross product per capita, but also of indices of infant mortality, illiteracy, and per capita daily caloric intake.

It is recognized that, in order to reach these objectives within a reasonable time, the rate of economic growth in any country of Latin America should be not less than 2.5 per cent per capita per year, and that each participating country should determine its own growth target in the light of its stage of social and economic evolution, resource endowment, and ability to mobilize national efforts for development.

2. To make the benefits of economic progress available to all citizens of all economic and social groups through a more equitable distribution of national income, raising more rapidly the income and standard of living of the needier sectors of the population, at the same time that a higher proportion of the national product is devoted to investment.

3. To achieve balanced diversification in national economic structures, both regional and functional, making them increasingly free from dependence on the export of a limited number of primary products and the importation of capital goods while attaining stability in the prices of exports or in income derived from exports.

4. To accelerate the process of rational industrialization so as to increase the productivity of the economy as a whole, taking full advantage of the talents and energies of both the private and public sectors, utilizing the natural resources of the country and providing productive and remunerative employment for unemployed or part-time workers. Within this process of industrialization, special attention should be given to the establishment and development of capital-goods industries.

5. To raise greatly the level of agricultural productivity and output and to improve related storage, transportation, and marketing services.

6. To encourage, in accordance with the characteristics of each country, programs of comprehensive agrarian reform leading to the effective transformation, where required, of unjust structures and systems of land tenure and use, with a view to replacing latifundia and dwarf holdings by an equitable system of land tenure so that, with the help of timely and adequate credit, technical assistance and facilities for the marketing and distribution of products, the land will become for the man who works it the basis of his economic stability, the foundation of his increasing welfare, and the guarantee of his freedom and dignity.

7. To eliminate adult illiteracy and by 1970 to assure, as a minimum, access to six years of primary education for each school-age child in Latin America; to modernize and expand vocational, technical, secondary and higher educational and training facilities; to strengthen the capacity for basic and applied research; and to provide the competent personnel required in rapidly-growing societies.

8. To increase life expectancy at birth by a minimum of five years, and to increase the ability to learn and produce,

by improving individual and public health. To attain this goal it will be necessary, among other measures, to provide adequate potable water supply and sewage disposal to not less than 70 per cent of the urban and 50 per cent of the rural population; to reduce the present mortality rate of children less than five years of age by at least one-half; to control the more serious communicable diseases, according to their importance as a cause of sickness, disability, and death; to eradicate those illnesses, especially malaria, for which effective techniques are known; to improve nutrition; to train medical and health personnel to meet at least minimum requirements; to improve basic health services at national and local levels; and to intensify scientific research and apply its results more fully and effectively to the prevention and cure of illness.

9. To increase the construction of low-cost houses for low-income families in order to replace inadequate and deficient housing and to reduce housing shortages; and to provide necessary public services to both urban and rural centers of population.

10. To maintain stable price levels, avoiding inflation or deflation and the consequent social hardships and maldistribution of resources, always bearing in mind the necessity of maintaining an adequate rate of economic growth.

11. To strengthen existing agreements on economic integration, with a view to the ultimate fulfillment of aspirations for a Latin American common market that will expand and diversify trade among the Latin American countries and thus contribute to the economic growth of the region.

12. To develop cooperative programs designed to prevent the harmful effects of excessive fluctuations in the foreign exchange earnings derived from exports of primary prod-

ucts, which are of vital importance to economic and social development; and to adopt the measures necessary to facilitate the access of Latin American exports to international markets.

TITLE II. ECONOMIC AND SOCIAL DEVELOPMENT

Chapter I. Basic Requirements for Economic and Social Development

The American republics recognize that to achieve the foregoing goals it will be necessary:

1. That comprehensive and well-conceived national programs of economic and social development, aimed at the achievement of self-sustaining growth, be carried out in accordance with democratic principles.

2. That national programs of economic and social development be based on the principle of self-help—as established in the Act of Bogotá—and on the maximum use of domestic resources, taking into account the special conditions of each country.

3. That in the preparation and execution of plans for economic and social development, women should be placed on an equal footing with men.

4. That the Latin American countries obtain sufficient external financial assistance, a substantial portion of which should be extended on flexible conditions with respect to periods and terms of repayment and forms of utilization, in order to supplement domestic capital formation and reinforce their import capacity; and that, in support of well-conceived programs, which include the necessary structural reforms and measures for the mobilization of internal resources, a supply of capital from all external sources during

the coming ten years of at least 20 billion dollars be made available to the Latin American countries, with priority to the relatively less developed countries. The greater part of this sum should be in public funds.

5. That institutions in both the public and private sectors, including labor organizations, cooperatives, and commercial, industrial, and financial institutions, be strengthened and improved for the increasing and effective use of domestic resources, and that the social reforms necessary to permit a fair distribution of the fruits of economic and social progress be carried out.

Chapter II. National Development Programs

1. Participating Latin American countries agree to introduce or strengthen systems for the preparation, execution, and periodic revision of national programs for economic and social development consistent with the principles, objectives, and requirements contained in this document. Participating Latin American countries should formulate, if possible within the next eighteen months, long-term development programs. Such programs should embrace, according to the characteristics of each country, the elements outlined in the Appendix.

2. National development programs should incorporate self-help efforts directed toward:

a. Improvement of human resources and widening of opportunities by raising general standards of education and health; improving and extending technical education and professional training with emphasis on science and technology; providing adequate remuneration for work performed, encouraging the talents of managers, entrepreneurs, and wage earners; providing more productive employment for underemployed manpower; establishing effective systems of labor relations, and procedures for consultation and collaboration among public authorities, employer associations, and labor organizations; promoting the establishment and expansion of local institutions for basic and applied research; and improving the standards of public administration.

b. Wider development and more efficient use of natural resources, especially those which are now idle or under-utilized, including measures for the processing of raw materials.

c. The strengthening of the agricultural base, progressively extending the benefits of the land to those who work it, and ensuring in countries with Indian populations the integration of these populations into the economic, social, and cultural processes of modern life. To carry out these aims, measures should be adopted, among others, to establish or improve, as the case may be, the following services: extension, credit, technical assistance, agricultural research and mechanization; health and education; storage and distribution; cooperatives and farmers' associations; and community development.

d. More effective, rational and equitable mobilization and use of financial resources through the reform of tax structures, including fair and adequate taxation of large incomes and real estate, and the strict application of measures to improve fiscal administration. Development programs should include the adaptation of budget expenditures to development needs, measures for the maintenance of price stability, the creation of essential credit facilities at reasonable rates of interest, and the encouragement of private savings.

e. Promotion through appropriate measures, including the signing of agreements for the purpose of reducing or eliminating double taxation, of conditions that will encourage the flow of foreign investments and help to increase the capital resources of participating countries in need of capital.

f. Improvement of systems of distribution and sales in order to make markets more competitive and prevent monopolistic practices.

Chapter III. Immediate and Short-Term Action Measures

1. Recognizing that a number of Latin American countries, despite their best efforts, may require emergency financial assistance, the United States will provide assistance from the funds which are or may be established for such purposes. The United States stands ready to take prompt action on applications for such assistance. Applications relating to existing situations should be submitted within the next 60 days.

2. Participating Latin American countries should, in addition to creating or strengthening machinery for long-term development programming, immediately increase their efforts to accelerate their development by giving special emphasis to the following objectives:

a. The completion of projects already under way and the initiation of projects for which the basic studies have been made, in order to accelerate their financing and execution.

b. The implementation of new projects which are designed:
(1) To meet the most pressing economic and social needs and benefit directly the greatest number of people;

(2) To concentrate efforts within each country in the less developed or more depressed areas in which particularly serious social problems exist;

(3) To utilize idle capacity or resources, particularly under-employed manpower; and

(4) To survey and assess natural resources.

c. The facilitation of the preparation and execution of long-term programs through measures designed:

(1) To train teachers, technicians, and specialists;

(2) To provide accelerated training to workers and farmers;

(3) To improve basic statistics;

(4) To establish needed credit and marketing facilities; and

(5) To improve services and administration.

3. The United States will assist in carrying out these short-term measures with a view to achieving concrete results from the Alliance for Progress at the earliest possible moment. In connection with the measures set forth above, and in accordance with the statement of President Kennedy, the United States will provide assistance under the Alliance, including assistance for the financing of short-term measures, totalling more than one billion dollars in the year ending March 1962.

Chapter IV. External Assistance in Support of National Development Programs

1. The economic and social development of Latin America will require a large amount of additional public and private financial assistance on the part of capital-exporting countries, including the members of the Development Assistance

Group and international lending agencies. The measures provided for in the Act of Bogotá and the new measures provided for in this Charter, are designed to create a framework within which such additional assistance can be provided and effectively utilized.

2. The United States will assist those participating countries whose development programs establish self-help measures and economic and social policies and programs consistent with the goals and principles of this Charter. To supplement the domestic efforts of such countries, the United States is prepared to allocate resources which, along with those anticipated from other external sources, will be of a scope and magnitude adequate to realize the goals envisaged in this Charter. Such assistance will be allocated to both social and economic development and, where appropriate, will take the form of grants or loans on flexible terms and conditions. The participating countries will request the support of other capital-exporting countries and appropriate institutions so that they may provide assistance for the attainment of these objectives.

3. The United States will help in the financing of technical assistance projects proposed by a participating country or by the General Secretariat of the Organization of American States for the purpose of:

a. Providing experts contracted in agreement with the governments to work under their direction and to assist them in the preparation of specific investment projects and the strengthening of national mechanisms for preparing projects, using specialized engineering firms where appropriate;

b. Carrying out, pursuant to existing agreements for co-operation among the General Secretariat of the Organization of American States, the Economic Commission for Latin America, and the Inter-American Development Bank, field investigations and studies, including those relating to development problems, the organization of national agencies for the preparation of development programs, agrarian reform and rural development, health, cooperatives, housing, education and professional training, and taxation and tax administration; and

c. Convening meetings of experts and officials on development and related problems.

The governments or above mentioned organizations should, when appropriate, seek the cooperation of the United Nations and its specialized agencies in the execution of these activities.

4. The participating Latin American countries recognize that each has in varying degree a capacity to assist fellow republics by providing technical and financial assistance. They recognize that this capacity will increase as their economies grow. They therefore affirm their intention to assist fellow republics increasingly as their individual circumstances permit.

Chapter V. Organization and Procedures

1. In order to provide technical assistance for the formulation of development programs, as may be requested by participating nations, the Organization of American States, the Economic Commission for Latin America, and the Inter-American Development Bank will continue and strengthen their agreements for coordination in this field, in order to have available a group of programming experts whose services can be used to facilitate the implementation of this

Charter. The participating countries will also seek an intensification of technical assistance from the specialized agencies of the United Nations for the same purpose.

2. The Inter-American Economic and Social Council, on the joint nomination of the Secretary General of the Organization of American States, the President of the Inter-American Development Bank, and the Executive Secretary of the United Nations Economic Commission for Latin America, will appoint a panel of nine high-level experts, exclusively on the basis of their experience, technical ability, and competence in the various aspects of economic and social development. The experts may be of any nationality, though if of Latin American origin an appropriate geographical distribution will be sought. They will be attached to the Inter-American Economic and Social Council, but will nevertheless enjoy complete autonomy in the performance of their duties. They may not hold any other remunerative position. The appointment of these experts will be for a period of three years, and may be renewed.

3. Each government, if it so wishes, may present its program for economic and social development for consideration by an ad hoc committee, composed of no more than three members drawn from the panel of experts referred to in the preceding paragraph together with an equal number of experts not on the panel. The experts who compose the ad hoc committee will be appointed by the Secretary General of the Organization of American States at the request of the interested government and with its consent.

4. The committee will study the development program, exchange opinions with the interested government as to possible modifications and, with the consent of the government, report its conclusions to the Inter-American Development

Bank and to other governments and institutions that may be prepared to extend external financial and technical assistance in connection with the execution of the program.

5. In considering a development program presented to it, the ad hoc committee will examine the consistency of the program with the principles of the Act of Bogotá and of this Charter, taking into account the elements in the Appendix.

6. The General Secretariat of the Organization of American States will provide the personnel needed by the experts referred to in paragraphs 2 and 3 of this Chapter in order to fulfill their tasks. Such personnel may be employed specifically for this purpose or may be made available from the permanent staffs of the Organization of American States, the Economic Commission for Latin America, and the Inter-American Development Bank, in accordance with the present liaison arrangements between the three organizations. The General Secretariat of the Organization of American States may seek arrangements with the United Nations Secretariat, its specialized agencies and the Inter-American Specialized Organizations, for the temporary assignment of necessary personnel.

7. A government whose development program has been the object of recommendations made by the ad hoc committee with respect to external financing requirements may submit the program to the Inter-American Development Bank so that the Bank may undertake the negotiations required to obtain such financing, including the organization of a consortium of credit institutions and governments disposed to contribute to the continuing and systematic financing, on appropriate terms, of the development program. However, the government will have full freedom to resort

through any other channels to all sources of financing, for the purpose of obtaining, in full or in part, the required resources.

The ad hoc committee shall not interfere with the right of each government to formulate its own goals, priorities, and reforms in its national development programs.

The recommendations of the ad hoc committee will be of great importance in determining the distribution of public funds under the Alliance for Progress which contribute to the external financing of such programs. These recommendations shall give special consideration to Title I. 1.

The participating governments will also use their good offices to the end that these recommendations may be accepted as a factor of great importance in the decisions taken, for the same purpose, by inter-American credit institutions, other international credit agencies, and other friendly governments which may be potential sources of capital.

8. The Inter-American Economic and Social Council will review annually the progress achieved in the formulation, national implementation, and international financing of development programs; and will submit to the Council of the Organization of American States such recommendations as it deems pertinent.

Appendix. Elements of National Development Programs

1. The establishment of mutually consistent targets to be aimed at over the program period in expanding productive capacity in industry, agriculture, mining, transport, power and communications, and in improving conditions of urban and rural life, including better housing, education, and health.

2. The assignment of priorities and the description of methods to achieve the targets, including specific measures and major projects. Specific development projects should be justified in terms of their relative costs and benefits, including their contribution to social productivity.

3. The measures which will be adopted to direct the operations of the public sector and to encourage private action in support of the development program.

4. The estimated cost, in national and foreign currency, of major projects and of the development program as a whole, year by year over the program period.

5. The internal resources, public and private, estimated to become available for the execution of the programs.

6. The direct and indirect effects of the program on the balance of payments, and the external financing, public and private, estimated to be required for the execution of the program.

7. The basic fiscal and monetary policies to be followed in order to permit implementation of the program within a framework of price stability.

8. The machinery of public administration—including relationships with local governments, decentralized agencies and nongovernmental organizations, such as labor organizations, cooperatives, business and industrial organizations—to be used in carrying out the program, adapting it to changing circumstances and evaluating the progress made.

TITLE III. ECONOMIC INTEGRATION OF LATIN AMERICA

The American republics consider that the broadening of present national markets in Latin America is essential to accelerate the process of economic development in the

Hemisphere. It is also an appropriate means for obtaining greater productivity through specialized and complementary industrial production which will, in turn, facilitate the attainment of greater social benefits for the inhabitants of the various regions of Latin America. The broadening of markets will also make possible the better use of resources under the Alliance for Progress. Consequently, the American republics recognize that:

1. The Montevideo Treaty (because of its flexibility and because it is open to the adherence of all of the Latin American nations) and the Central American Treaty on Economic Integration are appropriate instruments for the attainment of these objectives, as was recognized in Resolution No. 11 (III) of the Ninth Session of the Economic Commission for Latin America.

2. The integration process can be intensified and accelerated not only by the specialization resulting from the broadening of markets through the liberalization of trade but also through the use of such instruments as the agreements for complementary production within economic sectors provided for in the Montevideo Treaty.

3. In order to insure the balanced and complementary economic expansion of all of the countries involved, the integration process should take into account, on a flexible basis, the condition of countries at a relatively less advanced stage of economic development, permitting them to be granted special, fair, and equitable treatment.

4. In order to facilitate economic integration in Latin America, it is advisable to establish effective relationships between the Latin American Free Trade Association and the group of countries adhering to the Central American

Economic Integration Treaty, as well as between either of these groups and other Latin American countries. These arrangements should be established within the limits determined by these instruments.

5. The Latin American countries should coordinate their actions to meet the unfavorable treatment accorded to their foreign trade in world markets, particularly that resulting from certain restrictive and discriminatory policies of extracontinental countries and economic groups.

6. In the application of resources under the Alliance for Progress, special attention should be given not only to investments for multinational projects that will contribute to strengthening the integration process in all its aspects, but also to the necessary financing of industrial production, and to the growing expansion of trade in industrial products within Latin America.

7. In order to facilitate the participation of countries at a relatively low stage of economic development in multinational Latin American economic cooperation programs, and in order to promote the balanced and harmonious development of the Latin American integration process, special attention should be given to the needs of these countries in the administration of financial resources provided under the Alliance for Progress, particularly in connection with infrastructure programs and the promotion of new lines of production.

8. The economic integration process implies a need for additional investment in various fields of economic activity and funds provided under the Alliance for Progress should cover these needs as well as those required for the financing of national development programs.

9. When groups of Latin American countries have their own institutions for financing economic integration, the financing referred to in the preceding paragraph should preferably be channeled through these institutions. With respect to regional financing designed to further the purposes of existing regional integration instruments, the cooperation of the Inter-American Development Bank should be sought in channeling extra-regional contributions which may be granted for these purposes.

10. One of the possible means for making effective a policy for the financing of Latin American integration would be to approach the International Monetary Fund and other financial sources with a view to providing a means for solving temporary balance-of-payments problems that may occur in countries participating in economic integration arrangements.

11. The promotion and coordination of transportation and communications systems is an effective way to accelerate the integration process. In order to counteract abusive practices in relation to freight rates and tariffs, it is advisable to encourage the establishment of multinational transport and communication enterprises in the Latin American countries, or to find other appropriate solutions.

12. In working toward economic integration and complementary economies, efforts should be made to achieve an appropriate coordination of national plans, or to engage in joint planning for various economies through the existing regional integration organizations. Efforts should also be made to promote an investment policy directed to the progressive elimination of unequal growth rates in the different geographic areas, particularly in the case of countries which are relatively less developed.

13. It is necessary to promote the development of national Latin American enterprises, in order that they may compete on an equal footing with foreign enterprises.

14. The active participation of the private sector is essential to economic integration and development, and except in those countries in which free enterprise does not exist, development planning by the pertinent national public agencies, far from hindering such participation, can facilitate and guide it, thus opening new perspectives for the benefit of the community.

15. As the countries of the Hemisphere still under colonial domination achieve their independence, they should be invited to participate in Latin American economic integration programs.

TITLE IV. BASIC EXPORT COMMODITIES

The American republics recognize that the economic development of Latin America requires expansion of its trade, a simultaneous and corresponding increase in foreign exchange incomes received from exports, a lessening of cyclical or seasonal fluctuations in the incomes of those countries that still depend heavily on the export of raw materials, and the correction of the secular deterioration in their terms of trade.

They therefore agree that the following measures should be taken:

Chapter I. National Measures

National measures affecting commerce in primary products should be directed and applied in order to:

1. Avoid undue obstacles to the expansion of trade in these products;

2. Avoid market instability;

3. Improve the efficiency of international plans and mechanisms for stabilization; and

4. Increase their present markets and expand their area of trade at a rate compatible with rapid development.

Therefore:

A. Importing member countries should reduce and if possible eliminate, as soon as feasible, all restrictions and discriminatory practices affecting the consumption and importation of primary products, including those with the highest possible degree of processing in the country of origin, except when these restrictions are imposed temporarily for purposes of economic diversification, to hasten the economic development of less developed nations, or to establish basic national reserves. Importing countries should also be ready to support, by adequate regulations, stabilization programs for primary products that may be agreed upon with producing countries.

B. Industrialized countries should give special attention to the need for hastening economic development of less developed countries. Therefore, they should make maximum efforts to create conditions, compatible with their international obligations, through which they may extend advantages to less developed countries so as to permit the rapid expansion of their markets. In view of the great need for this rapid development, industrialized countries should also study ways in which to modify, wherever possible, international commitments which prevent the achievement of this objective.

C. Producing member countries should formulate their plans for production and export, taking account of their effect on world markets and of the necessity of supporting and improving the effectiveness of international stabilization programs and mechanisms. Similarly they should try to avoid increasing the uneconomic production of goods which can be obtained under better conditions in the less developed countries of the Continent, in which the production of these goods is an important source of employment.

D. Member countries should adopt all necessary measures to direct technological studies toward finding new uses and by-products of those primary commodities that are most important to their economies.

E. Member countries should try to reduce, and, if possible, eliminate within a reasonable time export subsidies and other measures which cause instability in the markets for basic commodities and excessive fluctuations in prices and income.

Chapter II. International Cooperation Measures

1. Member countries should make coordinated, and if possible, joint efforts designed:

a. To eliminate as soon as possible undue protection of the production of basic products;

b. To eliminate taxes and reduce excessive domestic prices which discourage the consumption of imported basic products;

c. To seek to end preferential agreements and other measures which limit world consumption of Latin American basic products and their access to international markets, especially the markets of Western European countries in process of economic integration, and of countries with centrally planned economies; and

d. To adopt the necessary consultation mechanisms so that their marketing policies will not have damaging effects on the stability of the markets for basic commodities.

2. Industrialized countries should give maximum cooperation to less developed countries so that their raw material exports will have undergone the greatest degree of processing that is economic.

3. Through their representation in international financial organizations, member countries should suggest that these organizations, when considering loans for the promotion of production for export, take into account the effect of such loans on products which are in surplus in world markets.

4. Member countries should support the efforts being made by international commodity study groups and by the Commission on International Commodity Trade of the United Nations. In this connection, it should be considered that producing and consuming nations bear a joint responsibility for taking national and international steps to reduce market instability.

5. The Secretary General of the Organization of American States shall convene a group of experts appointed by their respective governments to meet before November 30, 1961 and to report, not later than March 31, 1962 on measures to provide an adequate and effective means of offsetting the effects of fluctuations in the volume and prices of exports of basic products. The experts shall:

a. Consider the questions regarding compensatory financing raised during the present meeting;

b. Analyze the proposal for establishing an international fund for the stabilization of export receipts contained in the Report of the Group of Experts to the Special Meeting of the Inter-American Economic and Social Council, as well as any other alternative proposals;

c. Prepare a draft plan for the creation of mechanisms for compensatory financing. This draft plan should be circulated among the member Governments and their opinions obtained well in advance of the next meeting of the Commission on International Commodity Trade.

6. Member countries should support the efforts under way to improve and strengthen international commodity agreements and should be prepared to cooperate in the solution of specific commodity problems. Furthermore, they should endeavor to adopt adequate solutions for the short- and long-term problems affecting markets for such commodities so that the economic interests of producers and consumers are equally safeguarded.

7. Member countries should request other producer and consumer countries to cooperate in stabilization programs, bearing in mind that the raw materials of the Western Hemisphere are also produced and consumed in other parts of the world.

8. Member countries recognize that the disposal of accumulated reserves and surpluses can be a means of achieving the goals outlined in the first chapter of this Title, provided that, along with the generation of local resources, the consumption of essential products in the receiving countries is immediately increased. The disposal of surpluses and re-

serves should be carried out in an orderly manner, in order to:

a. Avoid disturbing existing commercial markets in member countries, and

b. Encourage expansion of the sale of their products to other markets.

However, it is recognized that:

a. The disposal of surpluses should not displace commercial sales of identical products traditionally carried out by other countries; and

b. Such disposal cannot substitute for large scale financial and technical assistance programs.

IN WITNESS WHEREOF this Charter is signed, in Punta del Este, Uruguay, on the seventeenth day of August, nineteen hundred sixty-one.

The original texts shall be deposited in the archives of the Pan American Union, through the Secretary General of the Special Meeting, in order that certified copies may be sent to the Governments of the Member States of the Organization of American States.

INDEX

* * * * * * * * * * * * *